EQ4 MAGIC

By Barb Vlack

EQ4 Magic

Acknowledgments

It takes a team to write a book. There is the writer and the editor (or two or three), the testers, the computer illustrator, the programmer, the beta testers, the food preparers, the house cleaners, the companions, those who sit and wait, and the friends who sit and listen.

Many thanks to **my husband, Dave,** for all his expert advice. He first introduced me to the computer and now keeps me supplied with the best equipment. He's there to solve my software problems and offer solutions. What a guy!

My son, Kevin, also supplied computer expertise, patient explanations, and mathematical calculations when I needed them. Thank you.

It's no secret among Electric Quilt software users who have used the various means of technical support that the staff at The Electric Quilt Company is fantastic. Working with them to write a book has been such a great experience that I came back for seconds. Thanks to **Dean Neumann** for writing a program that encourages so much creative quilt designing and to **Ann Rutter** for her explanations that I could understand. Thanks to **Penny McMorris** for believing in me and encouraging me in many ways. Her assistance has been most valuable. To **Diane McEwen-Martin,** my editor, go heartiest congratulations for making my ideas work. Her guidance made this book writing a most pleasant experience. My appreciation goes to **Amy VonDeylen** for doing the illustrations and the layout. To **Sharon Chase** and **Margaret Okuley**, who tested everything to make sure I didn't leave any steps out of the procedures, I give warmest thanks. And, to **Lu Vandemark** and **Jan Nelson** for their EQ support, I thank you.

Thank you, too, to **all the members of the Info-EQ list** and to **the members of the EQ Club of The Quilt Studio** in Woodstock, Illinois. They all provided encouragement and willingness to test out ideas. Their questions could always be answered and spurred me to learn new things all the time.

I dedicate this book to the successful marriage of **my son Andy** and **his bride Erin**. Their wedding added some excitement to the production schedule of this book as I made the preparations for that special event a priority. The designing of their marriage quilt in EQ4 showed me new ways to use the program, which I have passed on to you in this book. May they have a love and friendship that lasts happily ever after.

CONTENTS

Chapter 1
Introduction

Chapter 1
Introduction

A Word from the Author

Within the '90s we have had Electric Quilt software to boost our quilt designing, enabling us to create quilts on a computer which we would never have designed on paper. Since we have such a powerful design tool at our fingertips, it's an adventure discovering new ways to use this program.

EQ4 Magic gives you the EQ4 tips and tricks I have learned by working with the program. As I often said about Too Much Fun! (my EQ3 design book), I spent 1000 hours researching and writing so you could save 975 hours and go stitch. My experience with this book is similar. All the lesson steps have been checked and re-checked. This should save you lots of trial and error time. I also hope the book's projects and instructions will inspire you to follow new ideas, and go beyond the covers of the book.

Before doing any other lessons, first do these two: "Using Advanced Drawing Features," and "Customizing the Drawing Toolbars." These add tools and menu features. Perhaps you won't need these, but you'll be ready if you do.

Next, notice that the lessons are divided into three levels: "Easy", "Intermediate", and "Advanced." "Easy" projects are for EQ4 beginners. They require little previous experience with EQ4. "Intermediate" projects are for those comfortable using EQ4, but who still need all the steps. "Advanced" projects are more complex block and quilt designs. The projects are more free form and creative. You must have a fair amount of EQ4 experience to do "Advanced" lessons.

These levels are meant to help you. I encourage you to skip around, rather than reading the book from beginning to end. Try a lesson, but if you find a level too difficult, drop back to an easier level. Please don't do Advanced lessons if you have difficulty with Easy lessons. Practice, then take on the Advanced level. I want this to be a "user friendly" experience for everyone.

Before trying my lessons, I strongly advise you to work through the EQ4 Getting Started manual that came with EQ4, as well as many recipes in the EQ4 Design Cookbook. Fran Iverson Gonzalez's book, EQ4 Simplified, can also be used as a stepping stone for learning a lot about EQ4 before beginning this book.

I hope EQ4 Magic can introduce you to something new in EQ4. I'm learning new tricks all the time, even after working extensively with the program. So think of learning EQ4 as a never-ending exploration.

Use technical support opportunities offered by The Electric Quilt Company. There is no reason at all for any question to go unanswered. Most users of EQ4, and computers in general, have access to the Internet. Use that resource to get to the Electric Quilt website. Links from there will open up surfing activity to visit maillists of people discussing EQ4, web sites of EQ users, lessons for using EQ4, and a forum for questions and answers. The Electric Quilt web site address is: **www.electricquilt.com**. It's well worth the visit.

"Magic" has always been my explanation for things I cannot explain. The lightbulb lights after screwing it in and flicking the switch because of magic. Things pop up on the computer screen because of magic. I have no idea what goes on between my fingertips and the screen, so it must be

EQ4 Magic 3

magic. EQ4 is full of magic tricks because it does things I cannot do easily any other way. I'm surprised and impressed with what happens with button pushing and combination clicking. I share the tricks I have honed so you can make them your own. I expect you can expand on my ideas and thereby make them grow. I like that concept.

Don your wizard's hat – it has to have appliquéd stars and a crescent moon – and get ready to create your own special magic. Oh, before you do that, put 10 casseroles into the freezer.

Barb Vlack

Using Advanced Drawing Features

Step 3

Step 5

Step 6

The Advanced Drawing Features are available for the user of EQ4 to set up when needed. It is assumed that the default settings for drawing in EQ4 will be enough for a beginner at using a computer quilt designing program. When more functions are required for complex drawing, they are available.

1   Click FILE on the main menu bar. Click Preferences from the drop-down menu.

2   Click the Drawing Options tab.

3   Click in the box next to Advanced drawing features to add a check. Click OK.

✦ **Note:**
The Constraint angle box is grayed out and is not functional. The number next to Maximum partition is for setting the upper limit for how many partitions and segments you may use to divide an arc or line. The default 20 is probably more than enough for most drawing. The Maximum grid box will let you set grids up to 14.

4   On the WORKTABLE menu, click Work on Block.

5   On the BLOCK menu, point to New Block, click EasyDraw.

6   On the BLOCK menu, click Drawing Board Setup. You will see two additional tabs in this dialog menu: EasyDraw and PatchDraw.

7   Click the EasyDraw tab. Take a look at the options offered here.

By default there is a check in the box next to Snap to grid. You may click this box to remove the check.

• You would want to use Snap to grid when you are drawing lines that need to conform to the grid setup.

• You would want to disable the Snap to grid when you are drawing lines that should not conform to the grid setup.

EQ4 Magic   5

In the outlined box titled Snap to Drawing, you will see checkboxes next to Snap to nodes and Snap to lines and arcs. Click to check or click to uncheck.

- You would want to use Snap to nodes when you are drawing lines between established nodes.

- You would want to use Snap to lines and arcs when you are drawing lines that should connect to a line or arc in places other than at a grid dot or a node.

There is a number box for Sensitivity in pixels, and 7 is the default number. A higher number increases the sensitivity. That is, if you increase the number, you can be farther away from a grid dot, node, line, or arc and your line will jump a greater distance to connect. Conversely, a lower number makes you get closer to the dot, node, line or arc as you are drawing in order to connect. Remember that a pixel is a very tiny thing, so we're not talking great distances here. You may not need to change the default number of 7.

The box with Node Select lets you click to select one or all. This is a tool that you could easily overlook if your attention wasn't called to it. It is a nifty thing to use when drawing some interesting blocks in EasyDraw. If you leave Select one as your choice, you will be in the normal mode. If you click Select all, you can have fun changing your drawing by stretching lines from intersecting nodes. See: DRAWING WITH NODE SELECT ALL.

The box with Node Size lets you choose Small or Large. By default, we have small nodes. If you set nodes in your drawing and need them to be larger so you can see them, you can click here. I find this most helpful especially when I am connecting nodes between concentric arcs, such as in a New York Beauty block.

8   Click the PatchDraw tab to see the features there (you may view and change these settings, even when you are not working on a PatchDraw block).

Step 7

Snap to Grid tool   *Snap to Node tool*   *Snap to Drawing tool*

Using Advanced Drawing Features

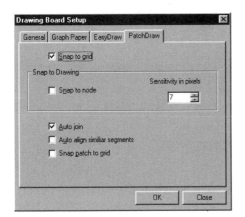

Step 8

Snap to Grid   *Snap to Node*
tool   *tool*

Auto Align Similar   *Snap Patch*
Lines tool   *to Grid tool*

Once again you will have a check next to Snap to grid by default.

In the Snap to Drawing box you have Snap to node and the Sensitivity in pixels, as you did above in EasyDraw.

Next you will see Auto join, Auto align similar segments, and Snap patch to grid.

- You use the Auto join tool when you are drawing line segments that you want to automatically connect with each other. For example, you are using the Bezier tool to draw several arcs that need to connect to form a patch. With Auto join, each segment you draw will snap and join to the next as long as you stay within the pixel sensitivity setting.

Trick:
It is recommended that Auto join be checked at all times. Remember that the goal for drawing in PatchDraw is to create a closed path (patch) by drawing one continuous curve, so you would always want this checked.

- You use Auto align similar segments tool when you have shapes with lines that will line up with each other. For example, if you took a 60 degree diamond shape from the Simple Shape tool and used Wreathmaker to make 6 diamonds in a wreath, you could enable this tool to help you align the diamonds to make a 6-point star. The Auto align similar segments tool is most handy for this job.

- You use the Snap patch to grid when you need to place shapes as you would for a pieced block. For example, if you have squares in PatchDraw that need to be set to conform to a grid, this tool will be helpful. The node that gets snapped to the grid is the node (in the patch) that is closest to a grid point.

EQ4 Magic   7

Customizing the Drawing Toolbars

It is very nice to be able to add buttons to the drawing toolbar (the column of tool buttons on the right side of your screen) to speed access to the various drawing tools.

Step 3

For EasyDraw

1 Click FILE on the main menu bar. Click Preferences from the drop-down menu.

2 Click the Drawing Options tab.

3 Click in the box next to Customize the drawing toolbars to add a check. Click OK.

4 On the WORKTABLE menu, click Work on Block.

5 On the BLOCK menu, point to New Block, click EasyDraw.

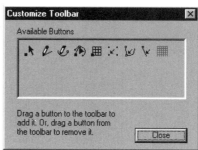

Step 6

6 Position your cursor on the right toolbar and right-click. A pop-out menu will display buttons for all the drawing functions for EasyDraw. Some of those buttons are not on the toolbar by default. You may add any or all of them to your toolbar.

7 Click the Snap to Grid button. Drag it over to the right toolbar and position it just under the Grid tool already there. You will see a dark line under the Grid tool when it is okay to release the drag. The Snap to Grid button will now be on your toolbar.

8 Click the Snap to Node button. Drag it over to the right toolbar as you did in step 7. Position it under the Snap to Grid button and release when you see the dark line.

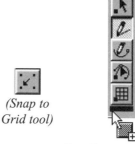

(Snap to Grid tool)

Step 7

9 Click the Snap to Drawing button. Drag it into position as you did in the previous two steps.

10 Click the Graph Paper button. Drag it into position. This button will allow you to hide or show graph paper as you need it for your drawing.

Name labels for these new drawing tool buttons are not available on the display menu.

Step 8
(Snap to Node tool)

Step 9
(Snap to Drawing tool)

Step 10
(Graph Paper tool)

However, once the buttons are on the right toolbar, you can rest your cursor over each button to pop-up the name. As the label appears for each button, you will also see a brief note about the function on the status bar at the bottom of your screen.

For PatchDraw

If you've already customized your toolbar for EasyDraw, you can skip to number 5 below. If not, begin with number 1.

1   Click FILE on the main menu bar and click Preferences.

2   Click the Drawing Options tab.

3   Click Customize the drawing toolbars (to place a check in the box). Click OK.

4   On the WORKTABLE menu, click Work on Block.

5   On the BLOCK menu, point to New Block, click PatchDraw.

6   Position your cursor on the right toolbar and right-click. A pop-out menu will display buttons for all the drawing functions for PatchDraw. You will see a few different buttons from those for EasyDraw.

7   Click the Snap to Grid button. Drag it over to the right toolbar and position it just under the Simple Oval tool already there. You will see a dark line under the Simple Oval tool when it is okay to release the drag. The Snap to Grid button will now be on your toolbar.

8   Click the Snap to node button. Drag it over to the right toolbar as you did in step 7. Position it under the Snap to Grid button and release when you see the dark line.

9   Click the Auto Align Similar Lines tool. Drag it into position.

10 Click the Snap Patch to Grid tool. Drag it into position.

11 Click the Graph Paper button. Drag it into position.

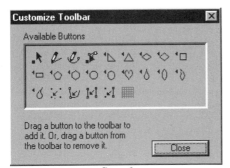

Step 6

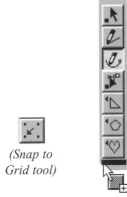

(Snap to Grid tool)

Step 7

Step 8
(Snap to Node tool)

Step 9
(Auto Align Similar Lines tool)

Step 10
(Snap Patch to Grid tool)

Step 11
(Graph Paper tool)

EQ4 Magic   9

Customizing the Drawing Toolbars

Editing Tools

There are three more helpful buttons you may opt to include on your toolbars. The editing tools will make the functions of cut, copy, and paste as easy as a pushbutton at your fingertips.

1   On the VIEW menu, click Edit Tools to place a checkmark. Three icons will appear on the left tool bar that should be familiar Windows™ icons for cut, copy, and paste functions. You can use these for copying and pasting (same as cloning) lines or shapes on the drawing boards, for copying and pasting information between Notecards in the Sketchbook or for copying and pasting text information from the Notecards into another program.

If you're curious, you may want to see what happens when you remove the check next to Project Tools in the View menu, but I don't know why you'd want to remove these. Just click to check Project Tools to get them back again. Ditto for the Status Bar.

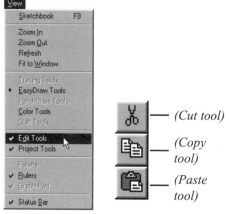

— *(Cut tool)*

— *(Copy tool)*

— *(Paste tool)*

Step 1

Chapter 2
Easy

Chapter 2
Easy

Making a Thousand Pyramids Quilt

Step 4

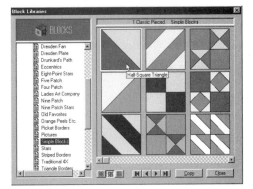

Steps 6-7

Step 9

One of the quilt layouts in EQ4 is Variable Point. This quilt layout offers diamonds on-point that you can skew by setting dimensions. One proportion that is a valuable dimension for these diamonds is 2 : 3.5. If you set the dimensions of the diamonds in the Variable Point layout, width being 2 (or multiples of 2) and height being 3.5 (or multiples of 3.5), you can have 60° diamonds that can be divided into equilateral triangles for a Thousand Pyramids quilt.

1   On the WORKTABLE menu, click Work on Quilt.

2   On the QUILT menu, point to New Quilt, click Variable Point.

3   Click the Layout tab and set any number of blocks horizontally and vertically.

4   For Size of blocks click, hold, and drag the slider bar button to set 6 for Width and 10.5 for Height (that's the 2 : 3.5 proportion multiplied by 3). Set sashing to 0.

5   Click the Layer 1 tab.

6   On the LIBRARIES menu, click Block Library. Double-click EQ4 Libraries if it isn't already open and double-click 1 Classic Pieced. Click Simple Blocks.

🖎 **Note:**
The pages are in alphabetical order so you may have to scroll down to see this category.

7   The first block is Half-Square Triangle. Click the block, click Copy, and click Close to close the library.

8   Click the Set tool. Click the Half-Square Triangle block.

9   Position your cursor on any of the blocks on the quilt worktable and press Ctrl+click to set the block. Move to any block that remains blank and Ctrl+click again so all the block spaces are filled.

10   Save in Sketchbook. Save the Project.

Making a Thousand Pyramids Quilt

EQ4 Magic   13

Making Hexagon Stars

Currently, "I Spy" quilts are very popular for children's quilts. The premise is to create a quilt gameboard with various novelty prints and challenge anyone to go on a scavenger hunt to find various objects. There are many good layouts for this type of quilt. Here is one using hexagons, that you can size any way you like, set with equilateral triangles.

1   On the LIBRARIES menu, click Block Library. Double-click EQ4 Libraries if it isn't already open and double-click 1 Classic Pieced. Click Simple Blocks.

🖐 **Note:**
The pages are in alphabetical order so you may have to scroll down to see this category.

2   Click the 4-block display button at the bottom-center of the Block Library. The Diagonal Strips block is now in the upper right corner. If you rest your cursor on it without clicking, the name of the block will appear. Click the block, click Copy, and click Close.

3   Click View Sketchbook. Click the Blocks tab if it isn't already open.

4   Click the Diagonal Strips block and click Edit.

5   Click the Select tool and click the long diagonal line in the block. Press the Delete key on your keyboard.

6   Save in Sketchbook.

7   On the WORKTABLE menu, click Work on Quilt.

8   On the QUILT menu, point to New Quilt, click Variable Point.

9   Click the Layout tab and make these settings by clicking the arrows or click, hold, and dragging the slider bar button:

   • Number of blocks Horizontal 4, Vertical 3

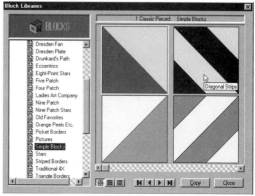

Steps 1-2

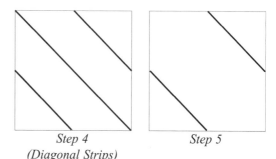

Step 4   *Step 5*
(Diagonal Strips)

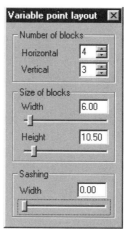

Step 9

Making Hexagon Stars

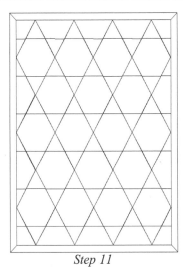

Step 11

Step 13
(Can you find the sunglasses, ghosts, cars,
ducks, and shoes?)

- Size of block Width 6, Height 10.5 (you must use the proportion of 2 : 3.5 to get a hexagon, but you may alter the size)

- No sashing

10 Click the Layer 1 tab. Click the Set tool.

11 Click the block you just edited. Position your cursor over the quilt layout and press Ctrl+click to set it into the quilt layout. Move the cursor to any block that remains blank and Ctrl+click again so all the block spaces are filled.

Trick:
If you rotate or edit a block line drawing on the quilt, be sure to hit the Refresh button on the left toolbar to get rid of previous lines.

12 Save in Sketchbook. Save the project.

13 Color the quilt with novelty prints if you like.

14 Save in Sketchbook. Save the project.

EQ4 Magic **15**

Drawing a 6-Point Star

Drawing an accurate 6-point star in PatchDraw is easy with the Simple Shape tool and WreathMaker.

ϟ Note:

For this lesson, make sure you have completed the two introductory lessons (USING ADVANCED DRAWING TOOLS and CUSTOMIZING THE DRAWING TOOLBARS).

1   On the WORKTABLE menu, click Work on Block.

2   On the BLOCK menu, point to New Block, click PatchDraw.

3   On the BLOCK menu, click Drawing Board Setup.

4   On the General tab, in the box for Snap to Grid Points, Horizontal divisions, type 48. Press the Tab key on your keyboard.

5   In the box for Vertical divisions, type 48. Press Tab.

6   In the Block Size, Horizontal, type 2. Press Tab.

7   In the box for Vertical size type 2.

8   Click the Graph Paper tab. Type 3 for both horizontal (press Tab) and vertical divisions.

9   Under Options, click the down arrow by Style and click Graph paper lines. Click OK. You will see graph paper lines dividing the board into a 3-grid (or 9-patch) block.

10   If the rulers are not showing on top and left of the drawing board, click VIEW, Rulers.

11   Click the black triangle in the lower-left corner of the Simple Shape tool. Click the 60 degree diamond. (Note illustration.)

12   Click the Snap to Grid tool. Be sure that Snap to Grid is the only snap-to tool enabled at this time. See: USING ADVANCED DRAWING TOOLS and CUSTOMIZING THE DRAWING TOOLBARS.

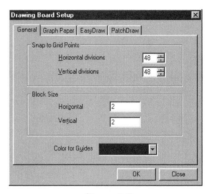

Steps 4-7

Steps 8-9

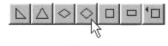

Step 11

Drawing a 6-Point Star

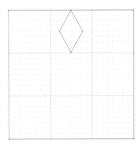

Step 13

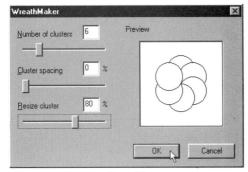

Step 16

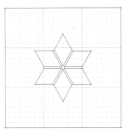

Result of Step 16

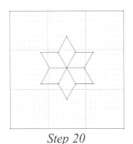

Step 20

13 On the drawing board, place your cursor at the 1" mark on the top line of the block and drag vertically for 8 grid dots. When you release the shape, it should fit from top to bottom in the middle upper square outlined by the graph lines.

14 Press the keyboard Spacebar to select the diamond you just drew.

Trick:
The shortcut to toggle between your drawing tool and the Select tool is to press the spacebar. You may also select the shape by clicking the Select tool and then clicking a line of the shape.

15 Right-click anywhere on the selected shape and a flyout menu will appear. Click WreathMaker.

16 Make these settings by dragging the sliding bars: Number of clusters 6; Cluster spacing 0%; Resize cluster 80%. Click OK.
You will now see a wreath of 6 diamonds with a small space between each diamond.

17 Clear the selection of the whole wreath by placing your cursor in a blank area away from the wreath and clicking.

18 Click the Auto Align Similar Lines tool on the toolbar and disable all other snap-to tools by clicking them to "turn them off". See: USING ADVANCED DRAWING FEATURES and CUSTOMIZING THE DRAWING TOOLBARS.

19 Click one diamond, hold and drag the selected diamond to line up with the nearest diamond to start forming the 6-point star. One diamond should be attracted to the other like a magnet. Be careful about alignment so the diamond centers meet.

20 Continue until all the diamonds are together and form the star.

21 Save in Sketchbook. Save the project.

Tip:
You may want to keep this block for future use. See pages 56-57 in the EQ4 Design Cookbook to add this block to the library.

EQ4 Magic   17

Making a Century of Progress Block

Pairing a 6-point star with other patchwork is easy with a block drawn in the Overlaid worktable (an applique drawing placed on top of a pieced block). For this example, let's draw the Century of Progress block that was first published in 1933 by *The Chicago Tribune*. The story is that the star represents the Star of Arcturus. Light from that star supposedly left the star in 1893, during the Columbian Exposition in Chicago, and was received here on Earth in 1933, during the Century of Progress, also in Chicago. I wondered if the great magician Harry Houdini might have been at either of these fairs, and found out a very young Houdini could have been at the Columbian Exposition (he was born in 1874) but he would have been more than legendary if he had been at the Century of Progress, since he died in 1926.

↟ Note:

For this lesson, make sure you have completed the two introductory lessons (USING ADVANCED DRAWING TOOLS and CUSTOMIZING THE DRAWING TOOLBARS).

1 Make a 6-point Star. Follow the lesson, DRAWING A 6-POINT STAR. Once you have the 6-point star on the PatchDraw worktable, continue with this lesson.

2 Click the Select tool.

3 Drag a square (marquee) around the entire 6-point Star to select the whole star.

4 On the EDIT menu, click Copy. You won't see anything happen, but you've placed a copy in memory.

5 On the BLOCK menu, point to New Block, click Overlaid. The Overlaid worktable lets us make a block combining applique and piecing. Click no to keeping the block.

6 Click the Applique tab at the bottom of the drawing board.

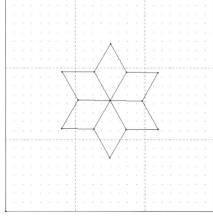

Step 1

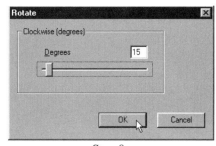

Step 8

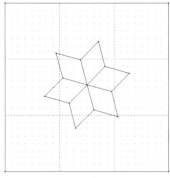

Result of Step 8

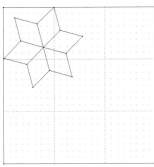

Step 9

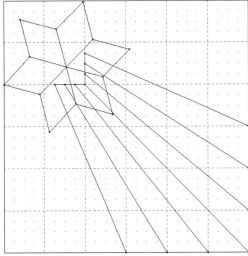

Step 15

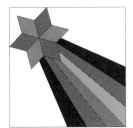

Step 16

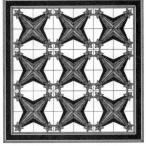

Quilt designed by Barb Vlack using the Star of Arcturus.

7 On the EDIT menu, click Paste. The 6-point star drawing will appear. If the middle lines of the star are not showing, click the Refresh tool.

8 Right-click on the star. Click Rotate from the pop-up menu. Type 15. Click OK. (Note illustrations on the previous page.)

9 Click, hold, and drag the star to fit in the top-left corner of the block. Set the block carefully so the points of the top and side diamonds of the star are touching the upper and left edges of the block.

10 Save in Sketchbook. Save the project.

Drawing the star rays in Pieced

11 Click the Pieced tab at the bottom of the drawing board.

12 On the BLOCK menu, click Drawing Board Setup.

13 Click the Graph Paper tab and set the number of divisions to 6 Horizontal and Vertical. Click OK.

Trick:
It is easy to advance from the Horizontal box to the Vertical box by pressing the Tab key.

14 Click the Snap to Grid button to enable it. No other snap-to tools should be enabled at this time. See: USING ADVANCED DRAWING FEATURES and CUSTOMIZING THE DRAWING TOOLBAR.

15 Click the Line tool. Draw lines as shown.

Note:
Count your lines. Be sure to draw 9 lines in all: 7 "Ray" lines and 2 short lines at the top of the "Rays." These top lines are crucial. Without them, your lines will disappear when you go to color your block. The patches in EasyDraw must be closed shapes, which are drawn by intersecting lines and lines that touch the edge of the block.

16 Click the Color tab, to color the block.

17 Save in Sketchbook. Save the project. Or, save the block in the Library.

EQ4 Magic **19**

Drawing with Node Select All

Hiding under an unassuming position in the Node Select box in the Drawing Board Setup for EasyDraw is tremendous potential for fun as well as serious quilt block designing. The default option for Node Select is Select one. The Advanced Drawing Feature is Select all. Here's how to use it.

↳ Note:

> For this lesson, make sure you have completed the two introductory lessons (USING ADVANCED DRAWING TOOLS and CUSTOMIZING THE DRAWING TOOLBARS).

1   On the FILE menu, click Preferences.

2   Click the Drawing Options tab and click to check Advanced drawing features. (If there is already a check mark in the box, you don't need to click it. See: USING ADVANCED DRAWING FEATURES.) Click OK.

3   On the WORKTABLE menu, click Work on Block.

4   On the BLOCK menu, click Drawing Board Setup.

5   Click the EasyDraw tab and in the Node Select box click Select all to put a mark in the circle. Click OK.

6   On the LIBRARIES menu, click Block Library.

7   Double-click EQ Libraries if this book is not already open and double-click 1 Classic Pieced.

8   Click Old Favorites.

↳ Note:

> The categories are in alphabetical order, so you may have to scroll down by clicking the down arrow to see this category.

9   The first block in the top-left corner of this category is Storm at Sea. Hold your cursor without clicking over the block to confirm the name and then click to select the block. Click the Copy button.

10 Close the Library by clicking Close.

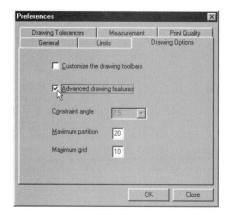

Step 2

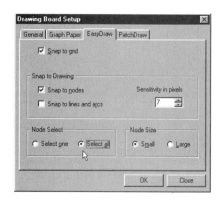

Step 5

Steps 6-9

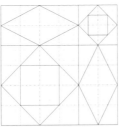

Step 11
(Storm at Sea block)

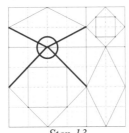

Step 13
(The lines have been darkened to emphasize the common lines of the circled node.)

The result of step 14
(Now Here's a Storm at Sea! block)

11 Click the View Sketchbook tool on the left toolbar. Then click the Blocks tab in the Sketchbook, the Storm at Sea block, and the Edit button.

Your Storm at Sea block is on the EasyDraw drawing board. Ready to play?

12 Save the block in the Sketchbook. You do want to save another copy of this block in the Sketchbook in order to establish nodes where lines intersect.

13 Click the Edit tool. Position your cursor on one of the intersections and click. You will see more than one line turn into a heavy dark highlight. Your cursor is at a node. Drag it in any direction and you will see all the lines drag with it.

14 Click another intersection and do this again. And again. And again.

 **Tips and Tricks:**

- If your next click retains a line that was involved in your previous step, simply click in a clear area on the drawing board to clear your cursor and go back to click the intersection again.

- If you click a node and only one line is darkened, click the Save in Sketchbook tool and try again.

- Yes, this node manipulation will work with curves, too, as long as you're in EasyDraw. This function does not apply to PatchDraw.

- As you move lines around to establish a new design, do consider the practical side, unless you know you would never in a millennium want to piece this block. Be careful to set up areas or units that could be pieced within your capabilities. Unless you like inset piecing, you may want to avoid arrow shapes. If you're clever, you could design this drawing to be foundation pieced.

- Save in Sketchbook any block design that has some possibilities. If you need to start over, you can go back into the Sketchbook, Blocks tab, click Storm at Sea, and Edit. Be sure to Save the project as well.

- You can set up an interesting quilt with this block. See: DOODLE QUILT DESIGN.

Flotsam and Jetsam Caught in the Propellers
An example of what can be made with the new block (it was rotated to create this quilt).

EQ4 Magic **21**

Making a Doodle Quilt Design

This formula for a nifty quilt design is based on the use of symmetry to rotate blocks and get secondary designs. It's a wonderful way to play with the Crazy Foundations blocks in the Paper Piecing Library.

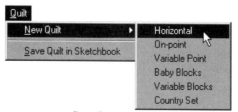

Step 2

1   On the WORKTABLE menu, click Work on Quilt.

2   On the QUILT menu, point to New Quilt, click Horizontal.

3   Click the Layout tab. Set the Number of blocks Horizontal to 4 by clicking the up or down arrow. Press the Tab key on your keyboard.

4   Type 4 for Vertical. Press Tab.

5   Type any number you like for a square block size (press Tab twice to change the height). The size won't make any difference until you are ready to sew the real quilt. Right now we're "doodling." Eliminate sashing by sliding the slider size bar until you get 0.00.

Steps 3-5

6   Click the Layer 1 tab.

7   On the LIBRARIES menu, click Block Library.

8   If the EQ Libraries book is not open, double-click it. Double-click 3 Paper Piecing.

9   Click Crazy Foundations.

10 The first block is Crazy I (you can hold the cursor over the block without clicking and see the block name). Click the block and click the Copy button.

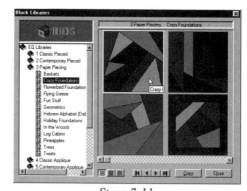

Steps 7-11

11 Click Close to close the library.

12 Click the Set tool.

13 Click the Crazy I block in the Sketchbook Blocks display.

14 Hold down the Ctrl key and click any block space to fill the entire quilt.

Step 12
(Set tool)

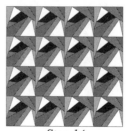

Step 14

*Step 15
(Rotate tool)*

The result of steps 15-17

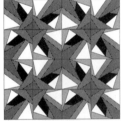

Step 19

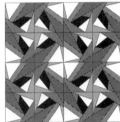

Step 21

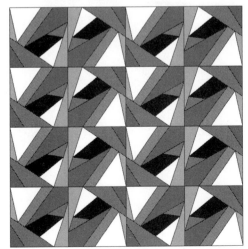

*Step 22
(An example using the
Rotate tool)*

15 Click the Rotate tool. Set your cursor on the second block from the top-left corner of the quilt and Alt+click. Every other block will rotate.

16 In the second row of blocks on the quilt, click each block two times. Each click will give you one rotation.

17 In the fourth row, click each block two times.

You will see an organization to your quilt that I find quite fascinating. You may have thought you were working with a crazy quilt layout, but there's something very special about this. Perhaps it's the surprise element. The surprise happens because you're working with asymmetrical blocks that have parts that could make stars or pinwheels as secondary designs when the blocks are placed in the quilt layout.

18 Save in Sketchbook. Save the project.

19 With the Rotate tool still selected, put your cursor on any block. Ctrl+click one time.

All your blocks will rotate once and you will see a different quilt!

20 Save in Sketchbook. Save the project.

21 Do steps 19 and 20 again. And once more.

22 Do Alt+click. Then do steps 19 and 20 again and again. You'll see even more quilts! You may get different results if you vary which block you select with the Alt+click. Experiment!

All you are doing is rotating a collection of 16 blocks here. Each rotation introduces a different symmetry. You may also flip some blocks (click the Flip tool on the right toolbar and Alt+click the blocks) and go through the whole process some more.

Go back and color your quilts according to secondary designs that might actually make the blocks disappear. *Now* you can color to make this beautiful! For dramatic results, use Designer Fabrics with a hand-dyed look. Try Lunn fabrics or Benartex Fossil Ferns. Add borders

EQ4 Magic   23

of your choice. I usually don't add sashing to this kind of quilt, but you may want to see what they do to your design. Sashing may actually look like an overlaid window with muntin bars.

Step 22
More examples of using the
Rotate and Flip tools

Drawing a "My Kind of" Beauty Block

There have been so many variations of the New York Beauty block recently that it would be difficult to pin down which one is the "original." I like the idea of having the variety to choose from. I like it even better that I can make up the block as I draw it in EQ4. This is an "Easy" drawing block in EQ4, even though the construction of the block may fall into "intermediate" or "advanced", depending on your favored technique. In EasyDraw, if you can draw a straight line, you can also draw an arc with ease. With the Partition editing tool, converting two arcs into a Beauty block is as easy as Presto! Change-o!

Step 2

🏹 **Note:**
For this lesson, make sure you have completed the two introductory lessons (USING ADVANCED DRAWING TOOLS and CUSTOMIZING THE DRAWING TOOLBARS).

1 On the WORKTABLE menu, click Work on Block.

2 On the BLOCK menu, point to New Block, click EasyDraw.

3 On the BLOCK menu, click Drawing Board Setup.

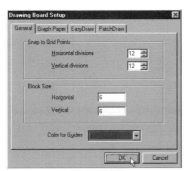

Steps 4-7

4 On the General tab, type in 12 for Snap to Grid Points, Horizontal divisions. Press the Tab key on your keyboard.

5 Type 12 for Vertical divisions. Press Tab.

6 Type 6 for Block Size, Horizontal. Press Tab.

7 Type 6 for Block Size, Vertical.

8 Click the Graph Paper tab. Type 12 for Number of Divisions, Horizontal. Press Tab.

9 Type 12 for Number of Divisions, Vertical. Click the down arrow in the Style box and click Graph paper lines.

Steps 8-9

EQ4 Magic   25

10 Click the EasyDraw tab. Under Node Size, click Large. Click OK.

🔖 **Note:**
You will see the EasyDraw tab if you have set up your Advanced Drawing Features in Preferences. See: USING ADVANCED DRAWING FEATURES **and** CUSTOMIZING THE DRAWING TOOLBARS.

11 If Rulers are not showing on the top and left of your EasyDraw worktable, go to the VIEW menu and click Rulers to check.

12 Click the Snap to Grid tool and the Snap to Node tool to enable them. The Snap to Drawing tool will not be enabled.

13 Click the Arc tool.

14 Position your cursor at the ½" vertical ruler mark near the top left side of the block and drag an arc to the bottom right edge of the block at the 5 ½" horizontal ruler mark, near the corner.

🔖 **Note:**
If your arc is not convex to the right, press the Spacebar on your keyboard before letting go of the drag and the arc will reverse its curve.

15 Drag another arc from the 2 ½" vertical ruler mark on the left to the 3 ½" horizontal ruler mark on the bottom.

16 Click the dark square in the corner of the Edit tool. A pop up menu will appear with the Edit Arc tools. In the box next to the word Partition, click an arrow to choose 5.

17 Click the arc on the left to select it and then click Partition in the menu box. You will see that the arc is segmented into 5 equal divisions with large nodes.

18 In the Edit Arc menu box, click an arrow to choose 5 next to the word Stagger.

19 Click the arc on the right to select it and then click Stagger. This arc will also be segmented in a different way than Partition. The equal division starts in the middle of the first segment.

Step 10

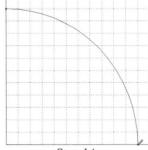

Step 14

arc tool

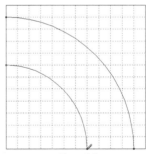

Step 15

Step 16

Step 18

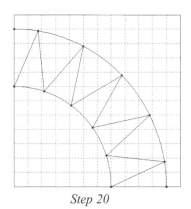

Step 20

Line tool

20 Click the Line tool. Starting at the bottom right corner of the left arc, play "Connect the Dots." Draw lines connecting the nodes on both arcs to get the triangle points of the Beauty block. You should have an arc with 5 triangle points evenly spaced.

21 Save in Sketchbook. Save the project.

 Tips and Tricks:

- Remember that if you make a drawing error, you can press Ctrl+Z to undo.

- This is a great block to use for gradations of values and colors. See: EXPANDING THE COLOR PALETTE.

Quilt design using the beauty block named Native American Beauty by Barb Vlack.

Drawing a "My Kind of" Beauty Block

EQ4 Magic 27

Setting Flying Geese in the Sashing

In the EQ4 Block Library there are many different patchwork blocks that will work quite effectively to make a pieced sashing. In EQ4 it's quite easy to set geometric blocks into the sashing and cornerstones to achieve magnificent results.

Let's try setting traditional Flying Geese into the sashing in a quilt with 12" blocks. We have to do some figuring (see how I avoided using the M for "math" word?) about how many geese in the proportion of 2:1 we need here. To sash the 12" block, we would need twelve geese 1" wide and 2" tall or six geese 2" wide and 4" tall. My choice is the six geese.

There is no block in the EQ Libraries with 6 geese, so you'll have to draw it.

⚡ Note:

For this lesson, make sure you have completed the two introductory lessons (USING ADVANCED DRAWING TOOLS and CUSTOMIZING THE DRAWING TOOLBARS).

1   On the WORKTABLE menu, click Work on Block.

2   On the BLOCK menu, point to New Block, click EasyDraw.

3   On the BLOCK menu, click Drawing Board Setup.

4   For the Snap to Grid Points, type in 6 for Horizontal divisions. Press the Tab key on the keyboard. Type in 6 for Vertical. Press Tab.

5   Type in 6 for Block Size Horizontal. Press Tab. Type in 6 for Vertical. Click OK.

6   Click the dark square in the lower left corner of the Grid tool. Click the arrow to set 6 in the box next to Columns. Click the arrow to set 1 in the box next to Rows.

7   Make sure the Snap to Grid tool is selected. Do not enable other snap to buttons at this time. See: USING ADVANCED DRAWING TOOLS and CUSTOMIZING THE DRAWING TOOLBARS.

Step 2

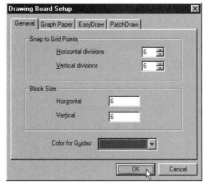

Steps 3-5

Step 6

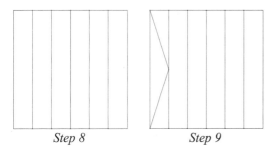

Step 8   *Step 9*

Step 12

Step 11
(Copy Button)

Step 12
(Paste Button)

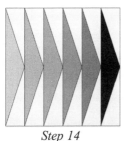

Step 14

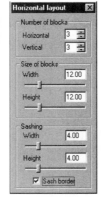

Step 16

Step 17

8 Drag a grid from the upper left corner of the block on the worktable to the lower right corner. You should only see vertical lines.

9 Click the Line tool. Draw the goose triangle as shown in the illustration.

10 Click the Select tool. Hold down the Shift key and click the two lines you just drew.

11 Click the Copy button.

Note:
If you don't have the Copy button showing on your left toolbar, go to the VIEW menu and click Edit tools.

12 Click the Paste button and move the lines into position to form the second goose.

13 Repeat steps 11 and 12 until all six geese are in line.

14 Click the Color tab. Color the block. Save in Sketchbook.

Trick:
Here is a wonderful place to try new colors.
See: EXPANDING THE COLOR PALETTE.

15 On the WORKTABLE menu, click Work on Quilt.

16 On the QUILT menu, point to New Quilt, click Horizontal.

17 Click the Layout tab and make these settings:

- Number of blocks: Horizontal 3, Vertical 3
- Size of blocks: Width 12.00, Height 12.00
- Sashing: Width 4, Height 4
- Click Sash border (so there is a check).

18 Click Layer 1 and be sure the Set tool is enabled. Click the Six Flying Geese block. Click the arrows on the sketchbook to choose the colored version of the block.

Setting Flying Geese in the Sashing

EQ4 Magic **29**

19 Position your cursor on a horizontal sashing strip and Ctrl+click. Do the same on a vertical sashing strip.

20 Click the Rotate tool on the right toolbar. Position your cursor on a vertical sashing strip. With Ctrl+click you'll rotate all the verticals simultaneously.

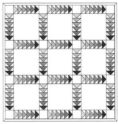

Steps 19-20

Tips and Tricks:

- I used the Diamond in the Square block from the EQ Library, 1 Classic Pieced, Diamond in Square, for the cornerstones of the sashing.

- Pick a classic block to set with the Flying Geese. Do not pick one that is too busy or the design of the block will conflict with the sashing. It's good for the design if you choose either an appliqué block for this setting or a block that repeats the triangle shape of the geese. I used the Oak Leaf Wreath III found in the EQ Library, 4 Classic Applique, Crossing Designs.

- You can place stars in sashing. See: MAKING A STAR SASH QUILT.

Diamond in the Square block

Setting Flying Geese in the Sashing

Barb's Flying Geese in the Sashing Quilt

Making a Watermelon Slice Wreath

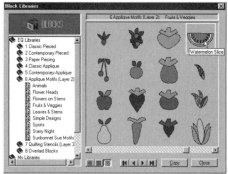

Steps 1-5

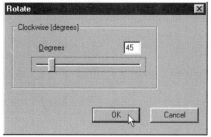

Step 10

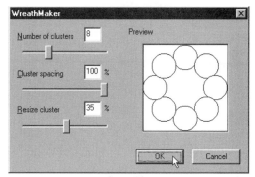

Step 12

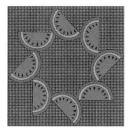

Step 13

1   On the LIBRARIES menu, click Block Library.

2   Double-click EQ Libraries if that book is not open. Double-click 6 Applique Motifs, then click Fruits & Veggies.

3   You will see a set of three buttons at the bottom left below the block display. Click the right button to display 16 blocks at one time.

4   Click the Watermelon Slice block that is in the top-right corner (hold your cursor over the block for a second without clicking and the name of the block will appear).

5   Click Copy. Click Close.

6   Click the View Sketchbook button and the Blocks tab in the Sketchbook.

7   Click the Watermelon Slice block and click Edit.

8   Press Ctrl+A on your keyboard to select the entire watermelon slice.

9   Right-click with your mouse. (You may have to double right-click.) Click Rotate on the pop-up menu.

10 Type 45 on the Rotate menu and click OK.

11 Right-click with your mouse again. Click Wreathmaker on the pop-up menu.

12 Set the Wreathmaker as follows:
    • Type 8 in Number of clusters. Press the Tab key on the keyboard twice.

    • Type 100 in Cluster spacing. Press Tab twice.

    • Type 35 in Resize cluster. Click OK.

13 Click the Color tab. Color your watermelon slice wreath.

14 Save in Sketchbook. Save the project. You can add a background to this applique motif if you want. See: ADDING A PATCHDRAW BACKGROUND.

EQ4 Magic   31

Adding a PatchDraw Background

Adding a PatchDraw Background

Applique motifs are wonderful additions to a quilt on Layer 2. If you want to use the motif as a block on Layer 1, you just add a background.

1   With the motif you want to add a background to in the Sketchbook (copy it from the Block Library), click Edit.

2   Press Ctrl+A on your keyboard to select all the patches in the applique motif.

3   Click the EDIT menu, click Copy.

4   On the BLOCK menu, point to New Block, click PatchDraw.

5   Click the EDIT menu, click Paste.

6   With the motif selected, click, hold, and drag the cross-arrows in the middle of the pasted motif to set/place the motif whereever you want within the borders of the block.

7   Click the Color tab and color the block. (When you Copy and Paste, EQ4 copies the design, not the color.)

8   Save in Sketchbook. Save the Project.

Tips and Tricks:

- The background for a PatchDraw block is considered a patch since it can be altered or removed.

Step 1

Step 1

Step 3

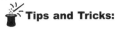

Step 4

Step 5

Steps 7

Making a Holly Wreath

Steps 1-5

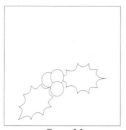

Step 11

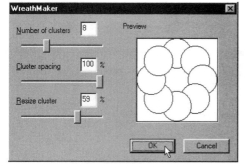

Step 14

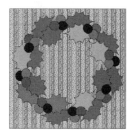

Step 15

1   On the LIBRARIES menu, click Block Library.

2   Double-click EQ Libraries if that book is not open. Double-click 5 Contemporary Applique, then click Christmas.

3   You will see a set of three buttons at the bottom left below the block display. Click the right button to display 16 blocks at one time.

4   Click the Holly block that is at the bottom of the third column (hold your cursor over the block for a second without clicking and the name of the block will appear).

5   Click Copy. Click Close.

6   Click the View Sketchbook button and the Blocks tab in the Sketchbook.

7   Click the Holly block and click Edit.

8   Click the Select tool and click the top holly leaf.

9   Right-click with your mouse. Click Rotate on the pop-up menu.

10 Type 45 on the Rotate menu and click OK.

11 Click, hold, and drag the leaf as illustrated.

12 With the holly leaf still selected, press and hold your Shift key on your keyboard and click the other leaf and the three berries.

13 Right-click with your mouse. Click Wreathmaker on the pop-up menu.

14 Set the Wreathmaker as follows:
    - Type 8 in Number of clusters. Press your keyboard Tab key twice.
    - Type 100 in Cluster spacing. Press Tab twice.
    - Type 59 in Resize cluster. Click OK.

15 Click the Color tab. Color your holly wreath.

16 Save in Sketchbook. Save the project.

EQ4 Magic   33

Making a Della Robia Wreath

1 On the LIBRARIES menu, click Block Library.

2 Double-click EQ Libraries if that book is not open. Double-click 6 Applique Motifs, then click Fruits & Veggies.

3 Click and Copy the Apple, Pear, and Grapes motifs. Hold your cursor over the block for a second without clicking and the name of the block will appear. Click Close.

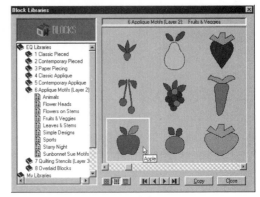

Steps 1-3

4 Click the View Sketchbook button and the Blocks tab in the Sketchbook.

5 Click the Apple motif and click Edit.

6 Press Ctrl+A on your keyboard to select the entire apple motif.

7 Right-click on the drawing board and click Resize.

8 Type in 50 for Horizontal and press twice on the Tab key on your keyboard.

9 Type 50 for Vertical and click OK.

10 Save in Sketchbook.

Step 5   *Result of steps 7-9*

11 Click View Sketchbook, click the Pear motif, and click Edit.

12 Repeat steps 6-10.

13 With the Pear motif selected, press Ctrl+C on your keyboard to copy to the clipboard.

14 Click View Sketchbook and click the resized apple motif. Click Edit.

15 Press Ctrl+V to paste the Pear motif on the drawing board.

16 With the pear selected, click, hold, and drag the cross-arrows in the middle of the pasted motif to position it slightly overlapping the apple on the right as in the illustration.

17 Save in Sketchbook. Save the project.

18 Click View Sketchbook, click the Grapes motif, and click Edit.

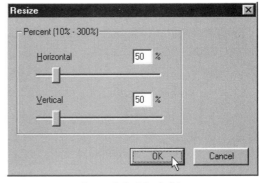

Steps 7-9, 12, & 21

Step 16

Step 20 *Step 21*

Step 27

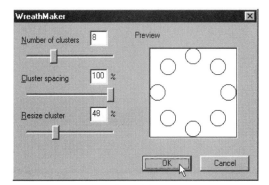

Step 30

Step 30

Step 31

19 Press Ctrl+A. Right-click with the cursor on the drawing board and click Rotate.

20 Type 45 and click OK.

21 Repeat steps 6-10.

22 Save in Sketchbook.

23 With the grapes selected, press Ctrl+C.

24 Click View Sketchbook, click the block with the apple and the pear, and click Edit.

25 Press Ctrl+V to paste the grapes onto the drawing board with the apple and pear.

27 With the grapes selected, click, hold, and drag the cross-arrows in the middle of the pasted motif to the left of the apple and slightly overlap. See the illustration for suggested placement.

28 Save in Sketchbook. Save the project.

29 Press Ctrl+A. Right-click on the drawing board and click Wreathmaker.

30 Set the Wreathmaker as follows:

- Type 8 in Number of clusters. Press your keyboard Tab key twice.

- Type 100 in Cluster spacing. Press Tab twice.

- Type 48 in Resize cluster. Click OK.

31 Click the Color tab and color your della Robia wreath.

32 Save in Sketchbook. Save the project. You can add a background to your current applique motif if you want. See: ADDING A PATCHDRAW BACKGROUND.

You may want to re-order the stacking of the applique patches.

Do it this way:

- Click the Select tool.

- Click the patch you want to restack.

- Right-click on the drawing board and click Send to Front or Send to Back.

EQ4 Magic 35

Making a Della Robia Wreath

Making a Folk Art Applique Wreath

1 On the WORKTABLE menu, click Work on Block.

2 On the BLOCK menu, point to New Block, click PatchDraw.

3 On the right toolbar, click the dark triangle in the bottom-left corner of the Simple Oval tool.

Step 3

4 Click the heart shape on the pop-out menu.

5 Click, hold, and drag a heart that is about one half the length of the block.

6 Click the triangle in the corner of the Simple Oval tool again and click the circle in the pop-out menu.

Step 5   *Step 7*

7 Click, hold, and drag a circle on the upper-right side of the heart. See the illustration for a positioning suggestion.

8 Click the triangle in the corner of the Simple Oval tool once more and click the curved leaf shape second from the right.

9 Click, hold, and drag the leaf from the bottom point of the heart diagonally up and to the right.

Step 9   *Step 10*

10 Drag another leaf shape from the bottom point of the heart up and to the left.

11 Click the Select tool. Hold down the Shift key on your keyboard and click all 4 shapes. Release the Shift key.

12 Right-click on the drawing board and click Wreathmaker.

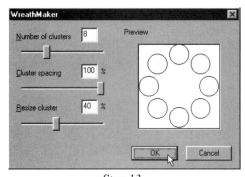

Step 13

13 Set the Wreathmaker as follows:

- Type 8 in Number of clusters. Press your keyboard Tab key twice.

- Type 100 in Cluster spacing. Press Tab twice.

- Type 40 in Resize cluster. Click OK.

14 Click the Color tab and color the block.

15 Save in Sketchbook. Save the project.

 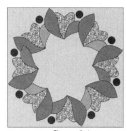

Step 13   *Step 14*

Can you see the difference in this block?
The large leaf was "Sent to Back."

If the block patches do not overlap, you can redo the drawing and make the shapes larger. Press Ctrl+Z to undo the last step and make the changes on the Wreathmaker menu or in your drawing.

You may want to re-order the stacking of the applique patches.

Do it this way:

- Click the Select tool.

- Click the patch you want to restack.

- Right-click on the drawing board and click Send to Front or Send to Back.

↳ Note:

If you send patches to back, you will be sending them behind the background of the block. To remedy this, select the background outline, right-click, click Send to Back.

EQ4 Magic 37

Making Round Robin Quilts

I love round robin quilts. They offer opportunities to try out new styles, use someone else's choice of color schemes, and share ideas with small groups of quilters. The concept is for a group of four or five quilters to agree to work together to add borders around a center medallion. Each quilter makes a center and gives it to someone else in the group. At the same time they are receiving a quilt. The assignment is to make a border for the quilt, hand it on to the next quilter, who adds another border, and so on until everyone has worked on each quilt.

Center medallion

In the real world, this round robin trading could take up to a year or more to complete in fabric. People do have their busy schedules.

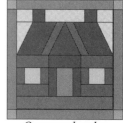

One new border

With EQ4, this same procedure can be followed using the program and email or a floppy disk. No fabric. No sewing. No year-long commitment. But no quilt to hang on the wall, either, unless you want to follow up and sew it. With this virtual round robin, a group of 4 or 5 agree to make a center and pass it on to the next person. You would have to structure the sequence so everyone has a chance to work on everyone else's quilt.

Two borders

Three borders

To send files to each other over the Internet, follow the procedure for attaching a file in your mail client program. Check with your Internet provider so that you know you can receive attachments. When you receive an attached EQ4 file, you can save it and open it in EQ4 as if you had drawn it there originally. You can design your border, save the file, and send it on.

I have seen this kind of virtual round robin take several weeks to complete. I have also challenged members of a round robin group to do all the rounds within a 24-hour period. It can be done. It's fun to do this as a relay race between groups. All it takes is a little organization and email.

Four borders and a great looking quilt!

Fruit Basket Block

Quilt Layout

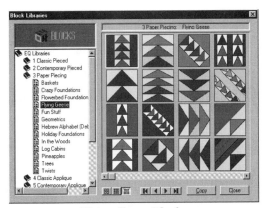

Flying Geese Blocks

Vine Block with Leaves and Berries

This is an example of a multi-border quilt that is a round robin quilt. The originator of this quilt made a center that ended up to be 17" with the plain strip around it to make the center block "float" away from the first border.

The center block was designed as an Overlaid block. The basket block is Fruit Basket from the EQ Libraries, 1 Classic Pieced, Pictures. The pieced basket block was copied from EasyDraw and pasted in the Pieced layer of Overlaid. The fruit came from Applique Motifs, Fruits and Veggies. The fruits were copied from PatchDraw and pasted into the Applique layer of Overlaid.

The quilt layout is Horizontal with one block. The block size is 14 inches.

The strip surrounding the center block is a 1.5" wide border spacer strip, Mitered style.

The pieced border is the Undulating Geese block from Sew Precise! 1-2, From Our Friends. It was drawn as a 7-goose block with the "noses" of the geese falling not in a straight line, so there's a wave formed by the blocks. You can also use the existing flying geese blocks in EQ4 or make your own. See: SETTING FLYING GEESE IN THE SASHING. The border is 2" wide, Rectangular Block style, with two blocks on each side. The corner blocks were drawn specially to coordinate with the Undulating Geese. They echo the shape of the geese and carry out the movement of the line.

The next border is another spacer strip that is 1" wide.

The appliqué vine border was drawn using the border stems and corners from EQ Libraries, 4 Classic Applique, Grape and Vine Borders. Leaves and berries were pasted into place along the vine, using automatic shapes in PatchDraw. The border is 5 inches wide and is a Rectangular Block style, with three blocks on a side. Note how the corner blocks connect the vines

EQ4 Magic 39

Making Round Robin Quilts

on the sides in a continuous line.

The outside of the appliqué vine border also has a 1" spacer strip to provide some separation between the vine and the pieced border.

The second Undulating geese border is also 2" wide, Rectangular Block style, 4 blocks on a side.

The last border is 5" wide, Mitered style. It has a quilting pattern that is from the Grape and Vine Borders book in 4 Classic Applique. It was set in Layer 3, so only the line drawing floats over the border background. The blocks were set and rotated so they provided a continuous line around the quilt.

The outside edge has a narrow border to look like binding.

The above explanation provided some insight into the designing ideas of the group that put together this round robin.

The borders around a center medallion tend to grow to be wider with each round. The border around the center will probably be the narrowest border in the series, and the outer border will be much wider. My guideline is to test to see what agrees with your designing eye. If your gut feeling says a border is out of proportion, it probably is.

Personally, I have found that alternating pieced and appliquéd borders is quite attractive. The curves of the appliqué provide a contrast to the geometric piecing.

Making a round robin quilt in fabric takes a great deal of careful measuring and often takes some tricky drafting to produce odd shaped blocks to fit. In EQ4, all that is taken care of automatically and the program will print out the patterns for you as well.

Layout for second Geese border

Finished Round Robin Quilt

Chapter 3
Intermediate

Chapter 3
Intermediate

Creating Stationery Letterhead

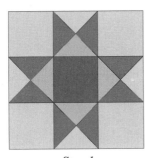

Step 1

Step 2
(Export Snapshot tool)

Step 4

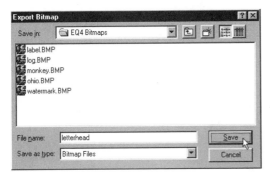

Step 5

Don't you love to use quilts or blocks to decorate your stationery? You can use EQ4 as a limitless resource to create graphics for an attractive letterhead - personal, professional, or surprise a friend. Happy letter writing!

Create a bitmap of a block or quilt

1 Have a colored block or quilt on the worktable.

2 Click the Export Snapshot button on the left toolbar.

3 A crosshair cursor will appear. Position the cursor at the top left corner of the block or quilt and carefully drag the cursor so the select box outlines the block/quilt and includes nothing else on the drawing board

4 Let go of your cursor and click Save as bitmap file on the Export Snapshot menu.

Trick:
If you make a mistake when you are creating the Snapshot, close the Export Snapshot menu by clicking the X and repeat steps 2-4.

5 An Export Bitmap dialog box will appear and you can name the file and save it where it is convenient for you to retrieve it later.

Trick:
I like to save these bitmaps in a folder of their own in EQ4. If EQ4 does not appear in the Save in dialog box, click the down arrow and navigate to find where you saved EQ4. Click the Create New Folder button and type EQ4 Bitmaps. Double-click this new folder (it will appear in the Save in dialog box). Place your cursor in the Filename dialog box, click, and type in a new name for your bitmap. Click Save. Every time I save an EQ4 bitmap, I open this folder and save it there, so all my bitmaps are in the same place.

Now we're ready to **open a Word document** and create our letterhead stationery.

1 In a New Word Document, click INSERT, point to Picture, click From File. Find your bitmap in the directory, select it, and click Insert.

EQ4 Magic 43

2 Click the picture. On the FORMAT menu, click Picture to get the pop-out menu.

3 Click the Picture tab. Click the down arrow next to Image Control, Color. Click Grayscale if you want to print without color. Click Automatic if you want a color printout.

4 Click the Size tab and use the arrows to size the picture (it will automatically resize proportionately). For this example, let's use a 1½ inch square.

 Trick:
If you want to stretch out the picture to fill your rectangular page, uncheck the boxes for Lock aspect ratio and Relative to original picture size.

Here the directions for Word 97 are different from Word 2000.

In Word 97:

A Click the Position tab. Click the box next to Float over text (so there's a check). Click the Wrapping tab and click Wrapping Style, Square. Click OK.

In Word 2000:

A Click the Layout tab and click Wrapping Style, Square. Click OK.

5 Click away from the picture to clear the cursor.

6 Click INSERT. Click Text Box. Click, hold, and drag a box on the right side of the picture. Release the mouse.

7 Type in your name and address.

 Trick:
If you are familiar with Word, feel free to experiment with the fonts, size, and alignment of your text.

8 The outline of the text box is selected and you may adjust the size of the text box to fit closely around the text. Hold your cursor over one of the white square nodes on the box outline. When the cursor is a double-headed arrow, click, hold, and drag

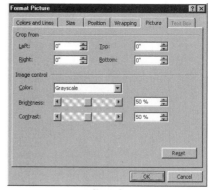

Step 3

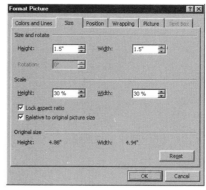

Step 4

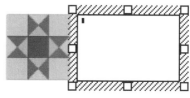

Step 6

Step 7

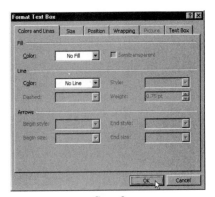

Step 9

Completed letterhead stationery

9 On the FORMAT menu, click Text Box, Colors and Lines tab. For Fill, Color, click the arrow and click No Fill. For Line, Color, click the arrow and click No Line. Click OK.

10 On the VIEW menu, click Page Layout. Click the text box to select it. (The page may already be in this view with the text box selected.) Position your cursor on the text box until you get the cross arrow cursor. Click, hold, and drag your text box if you want to change its position.

11 Select the graphic and move it into position as you did with the text box.

12 On the FILE menu, click Print Preview. Click Close. If the preview met your approval, proceed with the next step. If you did not like the preview, repeat steps 10-11 until you've positioned the text and picture where you want.

13 Save your letterhead stationery.

Tips and Tricks:

- This note assumes you placed the picture and text at the top of the page. When you begin typing text for your letter you will need to press the return key on your keyboard several times so your text is below the heading. Since we made the picture 1½" the text will need to be at least that far down on the page.

- You may want to Save As a document template for repeated use in the future. If so, in the Save As dialog box, click the arrow next to "Save as type" to get Document Template (*.dot). Type in a file name and click Save. Every time you open this template you should then save it as a Word document.

- You can make matching address labels. See: MAKING RETURN ADDRESS LABELS.

- You can make your own stationery where you can also use your letterhead. See: MAKING WATERMARK STATIONERY.

EQ4 Magic 45

Making Watermark Stationery

You can use Microsoft® Word 97 or 2000 to create your own watermark for stationery. A watermark is a faint drawing or text box that sits in the background on your paper. You can write or type text over it, and it will not be intrusive. This watermark can be used for decorative purposes or for security purposes, as in a notification of copyright or warning of confidentiality. Teachers may use this to designate their original material printed up as class handouts. Store owners may use this to put their stamp of identification on handouts from their store.

Step 1

Create a bitmap of a block or quilt

1 Have a colored block or quilt on the worktable.

2 Click the Export Snapshot button on the left toolbar.

Step 2
(Export Snapshot tool)

3 A crosshair cursor will appear. Position the cursor at the top left corner of the block or quilt and carefully drag the cursor so the select box outlines the block/quilt and includes nothing else on the drawing board.

4 Let go of your cursor and click Save as bitmap file on the Export Snapshot menu.

Trick:
If you make a mistake when you are creating the Snapshot, close the Export Snapshot menu by clicking the X and repeat steps 2-4.

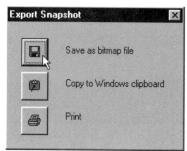

Step 4

5 An Export Bitmap dialog box will appear and you can name the file and save it where it is convenient for you to retrieve it later.

Trick:
I like to save these bitmaps in a folder of their own in EQ4. If EQ4 does not appear in the Save in dialog box, click the down arrow and navigate to find where you saved EQ4. Click the Create New Folder button and type EQ4 Bitmaps. Double-click this new folder (it will appear in the Save in dialog box). Place your cursor in the Filename dialog box, click, and type in a new name for your bitmap. Click Save. Every time I save an EQ4 bitmap, I

Step 5

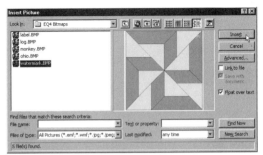

Step 1

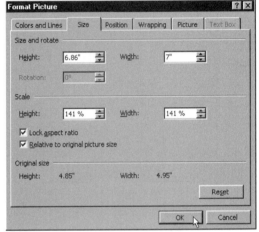

Step 3

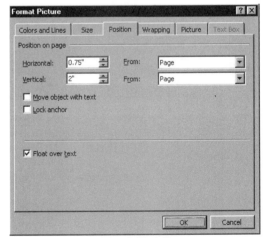

Word 97 A-E

open this folder and save it there, so all my bitmaps are in the same place.

Now we're ready to **open a Word document** and create our watermark stationery.

1 In a New Word Document, click INSERT, point to Picture, click From File. Find your bitmap in the directory, select it, and click Insert.

2 Click the picture. Click FORMAT, Picture.

3 Click the Size tab and use the arrows to size the picture (Horizontal and Vertical). It will automatically resize proportionately. If you want to stretch out the picture to fill your rectangular page, uncheck the boxes for Lock aspect ratio and Relative to original picture size.

Here the directions for Word 97 are different from Word 2000.

In Word 97:

A Click the Position tab. Click to place a check in the box next to Float over text.

B For Horizontal, click the arrows to get a number to center your block horizontally across the page. For example, if you sized your block or quilt to be 7" wide, and you're working with a page that is 8 ½" wide, make your number .75 to center (half the difference between 7 and 8 ½")

C Click the down arrow by From and click Page.

Trick:
When you click "From" and designate Page, the measurement you indicate will begin at the edge of the page, no matter what the margin setting is. The graphic can float into the text margins. Do not go closer than .5 or .25 "From the Page" or you will be overlapping the printing margins and your picture will be cut off.

D For Vertical, again consider the size of your block or quilt. If your block or quilt is 7" in height, and you're working with a page that is 11 inches tall, make your number 2" to center.

EQ4 Magic 47

E Click the down arrow by From and click Page.

F Click the Wrapping tab and click the diagram over None.

G Click the Picture tab. Under Image Control, click the down arrow and click Watermark. Click OK. Your image on the screen should be light colored and centered.

Word 97 F

🔖 **Note:**
Make sure the Drawing toolbar for Word is available. To make it visible, click VIEW, point to Toolbars, and click Drawing to check that option.

H Click the picture. In the Drawing toolbar, click the down arrow to the right of the word Draw (which is on the far left side of the toolbar), point to Order, click Send behind text.

In Word 2000:

A Click the Layout tab. Under Wrapping Style, click Behind text.

B Click the Advanced button. Under Horizontal, Alignment, click the arrow to get Centered. In the next box to the right, click the arrow to get Page. You will end up with "Horizontal Alignment Centered Relative to Page."

Word 97 G

C Under Vertical, click the arrow to get Centered and then Page. You will end up with "Vertical Alignment Centered Relative to Page."

D Click the Picture tab. Under Image Control, click the down arrow next to get Watermark. Click Watermark. Click OK. Click OK again.

Your image will be centered on the document page and will have a faint coloring. Test it by typing something on top of the watermark.

4 Save your watermark stationery.

Dear Amy,

Do you like my watermark stationery? I created it using the book EQ4 Magic – neat!!

See you at quilt guild,

Jan

Step 4

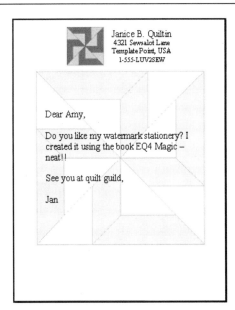

Janice B. Quiltin
4321 Sewsalot Lane
Template Point, USA
1-555-LUV2SEW

Dear Amy,

Do you like my watermark stationery? I created it using the book EQ4 Magic – neat!!

See you at quilt guild,

Jan

Janice B. Quiltin
4321 Sewsalot Lane
Template Point, USA

33¢

Amy Sunshine
1200 Bright Way
Sunbonnet, USA

Tips and Tricks:

- If you need to tweak the contrast or brightness click FORMAT, Picture, and the Picture tab.

- If your typing does not show up, it may be hidden under the watermark. Make that correction in FORMAT, Picture, and the Position tab for Word 97 or the Layout tab for Word 2000.

- If you want to change your watermark from pastel colors to gray scale, with the block selected, go back into FORMAT, Picture, Picture tab. Under Image Control, click the down arrow to get Grayscale. Click OK.

- You may want to Save As a document template for repeated use in the future. If so, in the Save As dialog box, click the arrow next to "Save as type" to get Document Template (*.dot). Type in a file name and click Save. Every time you open this template you should then save it as a Word document.

- You can make matching address labels. See: MAKING RETURN ADDRESS LABELS.

- You can make a personalized letterhead. See: CREATING STATIONERY LETTERHEAD.

Making Watermark Stationery

EQ4 Magic **49**

Making Return Address Labels

You can use Microsoft® Word 97 or 2000 to make sheets of mailing labels that will personalize your correspondence. There's more than one way to do this, but let me explain the way I found to work easiest for me.

To illustrate your mailing labels, you may choose to make a bitmap of a quilt, or a block you have assumed as your logo, or a collection of interesting blocks. If you choose a quilt, remember that you will be reducing it to about a 1" square, and a lot of the detail in the quilt will be lost. I suggest you choose one or more favorite blocks for this project.

Step 1

1   With a new EQ4 project file open, on the LIBRARIES menu, click Block Library. Go "shopping" through any of the libraries, and for each block you want to work with, click the block and click Copy. Click Close when you're finished.

2   Click the View Sketchbook button, click the Blocks tab, click a block to select it, and click Edit.

3   Your block will open on the drawing board. Click the Color tab. Color your block as you desire.

4   Click the Export Snapshot button on the left toolbar.

5   A crosshair cursor will appear. Position the cursor at the top left corner of the block and carefully drag the cursor so the select box outlines the block and includes nothing else on the drawing board.

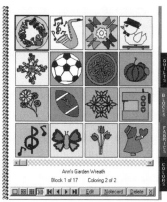

Ann's Garden Wreath
Block 1 of 17   Coloring 2 of 2

Step 2

Step 4
(Export Snapshot tool)

6   Let go of your cursor and click Save as bitmap file on the Export Snapshot menu.

 Trick:
If you make a mistake when you are creating the Snapshot, close the Export Snapshot menu by clicking the X and repeat steps 4-6.

7   An Export Bitmap dialog box will appear and you can name the file and save it where it is convenient for you to retrieve it later.

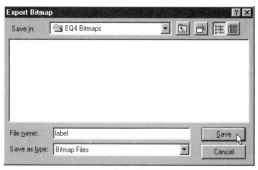

Step 7

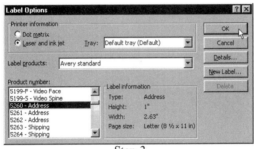

Step 2
(This is what you will see in Word 97)

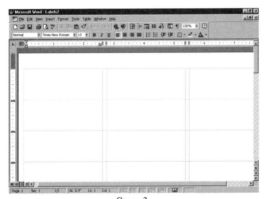

Step 3

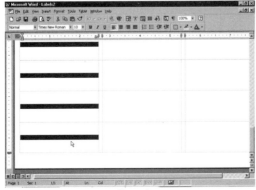

Step 4

🎩 **Trick:**
I like to save these bitmaps in a folder of their own in EQ4. If EQ4 does not appear in the Save in dialog box, click the down arrow and navigate to find where you saved EQ4. Click the Create New Folder button and type EQ4 Bitmaps. Double-click this new folder (it will appear in the Save in dialog box). Place your cursor in the Filename dialog box, click, and type in a new name for your bitmap. Click Save. Every time I save an EQ4 bitmap, I open this folder and save it there, so all my bitmaps are in the same place.

8   Repeat steps 2-7 for each block you want to use.

Now we're ready to **open a Word document** and create a sheet of mailing labels.

1   In a New Word Document, click TOOLS, click Envelopes and Labels.

2   Click the Labels tab and click Options. I like to use Avery Standard products, #5260 Address Labels. Click the down arrow by the Label products dialog box and click Avery Standard. Scroll the display box with the up and down arrows (Product number) and click the catalog number (5260-Address). Click OK. That will close this dialog box and show the previous one.

🎩 **Trick:**
These labels are not the small return address labels but rather the larger address labels. The block graphic shows up better on this size label. However, after studying this setup procedure, you may wish to adapt the directions to make the smaller labels.

3   Click the New Document button and an illustration of the sheet of address labels will be on your screen. Gridlines outlining the cells are visible.

🔌 **Note:**
To make the gridlines visible, click TABLE, click Show Gridlines.

4   Holding down the left mouse button, drag your cursor down the left vertical row to select it. You will see a thick black bar across the center of each of the labels in the first row. Release your mouse.

EQ4 Magic   **51**

5 Click TABLE and Split Cells. In the pop-up box, next to Columns, click 2. Remove the check next to "Merge cells before split." Click OK.

6 There is now a light vertical line dividing each of the labels in the first row. Click away from the first row to clear your cursor.

7 Position your cursor just a hair to the left of the vertical line dividing the top left label. Your cursor will turn into two vertical lines with arrows on each side. (This kind of cursor helps you move the line.)

8 Hold down your left mouse button and drag the line to the left so the left column is 1" wide. The ruler at the top of the worktable will be your guide.

✤ Note:
If you don't see the rulers to the left and across the top of your document screen, click VIEW and Ruler.

9 Follow the directions in steps 4-8 for the middle column and then for the right column of labels. The vertical line in the middle column should be parked at the 3 ¾" mark. The line in the right column should be parked at the 6 ½" mark. You have just created cells in a table.

To **set the picture** on the left side of each label:

10 Set your cursor in the left cell of the top left label and click. Press the Backspace key on your keyboard one time. (This puts your cursor closer to the edge of the label.)

11 Click INSERT, point to Picture, click From File. Find your desired bitmap in the directory, select it, click Insert. Your picture will appear and "magically" fit in the space.

12 Click the picture in the label to select it. Click the Copy button on the top toolbar (or click EDIT, Copy).

Here the directions for Word 97 are different from the directions for Word 2000.
In Word 97:

A Click the left cell of the second label in the

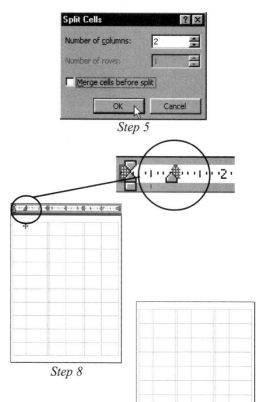
Step 5

Step 8

Step 9

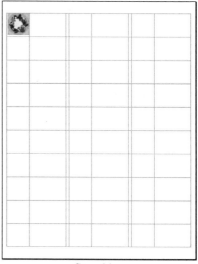
Step 11

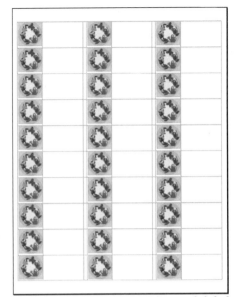

The bitmap has been pasted in each label

Steps 13-16

left column. Backspace one space. Press Ctrl+V to paste.

B Repeat this step for all the other left cells of the address labels. You must set them one at a time.

In Word 2000:

A Click the left cell of the second label in the left column. Backspace once.

B Hold down the left mouse button and drag to the bottom of the column. You will see the heavy black bar across the left space of all the labels in that column.

C Press Ctrl+V to Paste and the picture will appear in each selected space.

D Repeat this step for the entire center and right columns of labels.

Check to be sure the picture is close to the left edge of the label. Make adjustments with the space bar or backspace buttons if necessary.

To **set the address information** on the right side of each label in Word 97 and Word 2000:

13 Click the right half of the top label in the left column of labels. Your cursor will set itself in the center line of that space.

✎**Tip:**
I have found the following method of typing in the address works best for me. Follow carefully.

14 Press the spacebar one time. Type in name. At the end of the line, press Shift+Enter. This will take you to the next line without ending the paragraph.

15 Press the spacebar one time. Type in street address. Press Shift+Enter.

16 Press the spacebar one time. Type in city, state, zip. Do *not* hit Enter.

☆ **Tricks:**

• You may wish to edit the point size of the font to get all the name and address to fit properly on the label. I like to make the name larger and bolder than the rest of the address text. Be sure you select all the text after editing. If you want to add another line to

EQ4 Magic **53**

your text here, be sure to use the Shift+Enter key stroke and do not use Enter.

- In *Word 2000*, if the text is not centered vertically in the cell, you can fix that this way: Click on Table, Table Properties, Cell tab. Under Vertical alignment, click on Center. Click on OK. This may be necessary, since Word 2000 offers you more than one vertical alignment choice.

17 Click in front of the name in the first line (your cursor will be blinking), hold down Shift, click at the end of the text (to select it all).

18 Click the Copy tool (or click EDIT, Copy). Once again the directions for Word 97 and Word 2000 change.

In Word 97:

A Press the spacebar once and press Ctrl+V (or the Paste tool) to copy the text into each box individually.

In Word 2000:

A Select the entire column and press Ctrl+V (or the Paste tool) to paste. Set the text into the other two columns.

19 Save the document when you are finished.

 Tips and Tricks:

- You may want to print out a practice sheet of labels to check how they look before you do your final printout on a sheet of labels.
- If your printer tends to shave off the graphic on the left side of the label, you may need to move the vertical bar of the table to the right.
- Printing the labels in color is attractive.
- There are 30 labels on a sheet, and you can set different blocks into the left side of each label. Follow steps 10-11 for each label.
- Three or four colorful sheets of these labels would make a wonderful personalized gift.
- *Big tip:* You would follow the same procedure outlined above to set up business cards in Word with Avery product 5371.
- Make a sheet of larger labels for book plates for yourself or as a gift.
- You can make a personalized letterhead. See: CREATING STATIONERY LETTERHEAD.
- You can make watermark stationery. See: MAKING WATERMARK STATIONERY.

Steps 17-18
A finished sheet of labels

We're buzzin' about quilting!

Quiltin' B's
Bev, Beth, and Brenda
1234 Log Cabin Drive
Quilt Port, USA

A business card using the
steps in this lesson
(I used Avery 5371)

Drawing a Feathered Ohio Star

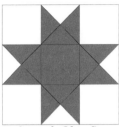

9-patch Ohio Star

One of the easiest Feathered Star patterns to draw in EQ4 is this Feathered Ohio Star. It is based on the 9-patch block, Ohio Star though it has an uneven patch grid to allow for the diamond points.

1 On the WORKTABLE menu, click Work on Block.

2 On the BLOCK menu, point to New Block, click EasyDraw.

3 On the BLOCK menu, click Drawing Board Setup.

4 In the box for Snap to Grid Points, Horizontal divisions, type 32. Press the Tab key on your keyboard.

5 In the box for Vertical divisions, type 32. Press Tab.

6 In the box for Block Size, Horizontal, type 8. Press Tab.

7 In the Block Size Vertical, type 8. Click OK.

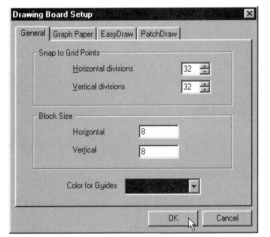

Steps 3-7

✎**Tip:**
The block size you set for drawing has nothing to do with the block size you use in the quilt or for patterns. Here it is only a setting of the Rulers for drafting.

8 On the VIEW menu, click Rulers to put a check. You will use the ruler markings for this drawing.

9 Click the Snap to Grid tool. No other snap-to tools should be enabled. See: USING ADVANCED DRAWING FEATURES and CUSTOMIZING THE DRAWING TOOLBAR.

10 Click the Line tool and draw a horizontal line across the block at the 2¾" mark on the ruler on the left side of the drawing board.

Step 10

Trick:
Remember that you can press Ctrl+Z to undo your line drawing.

EQ4 Magic 55

11 Draw vertical lines from the top edge of the block to the horizontal line at the 2 ¾" and 5¼" markings on the ruler across the top of the drawing board.

12 Save in Sketchbook. Save the project.

🖈 **Note:**
When you Save in Sketchbook, all lines drawn will be segmented where other lines cross or meet them. This is quite handy for some drawing requirements.

13 Click the Select tool and click the horizontal line segment on the right. Press the Delete key on your keyboard.

14 Click the horizontal line segment on the left. Press the Delete key. Click the Refresh Screen tool.

15 Click the Line tool. Draw a vertical line from the top edge of the block to the horizontal line ½" inside each of the vertical lines. Note illustration.

16 Starting at the horizontal line, draw three ½" lines to form squares in each narrow vertical column.

17 Draw diagonal lines across these three squares in each of these columns.

18 Draw diagonal lines AB across the figure.

19 **Important:** Save in Sketchbook. Save the project.

You have now segmented lines AB and created new line segments CD in the center column.

20 Click the Refresh Screen tool. Click the black square on the Edit tool to get the pop-up Edit menu.

21 Click each of the CD segments and click Half on the Edit menu. You are dividing these lines into two segments.

22 Click the Snap to Node tool. See: USING ADVANCED DRAWING FEATURES and CUSTOMIZING THE DRAWING TOOLBAR. Click the Line tool and draw a diagonal line from the upper-left corner of this figure to the middle of the right newly segmented CD line.

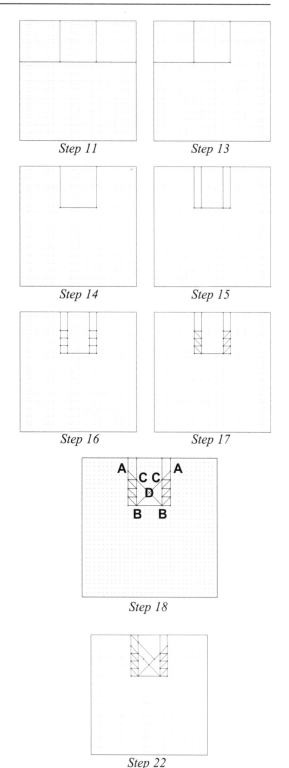

Step 11   *Step 13*

Step 14   *Step 15*

Step 16   *Step 17*

Step 18

Step 22

Drawing a Feathered Ohio Star

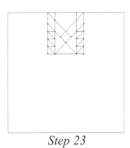

Step 23

Delete these two lines

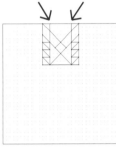

Step 25

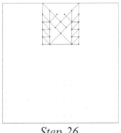

Step 26

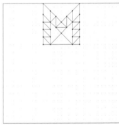

Step 27

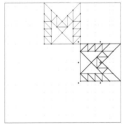

Result of steps 29-32

23 Draw another diagonal line from the upper right corner of this figure to the middle of the left newly segmented CD line.

24 Save in Sketchbook. Save the project. You should be able to identify where the corner diamond pieces will be, but you have an extraneous line extending from each of the inside vertical lines. Because you have segmented these lines with your saving in Sketchbook, they will be easy to delete. They did not disappear automatically with the save, though, because the lines connected to the edge of the block and did not end in open space.

25 Click the Select tool. Hold down the Shift key and click each of the two extra lines to select them. Press the Delete key on your keyboard.
You need just a few more lines before you're finished with this drawing.

26 Click the Line tool and draw lines to form squares on each side of the center square on point. In order to do this, you will have to extend your line beyond the line outlining the star so you can attach to a grid dot. That's okay. Save in Sketchbook, click the Color tab and then click EasyDraw and you will see that the line has disappeared. See the illustration.

27 Divide those last three squares into triangles by drawing vertical lines on the side squares and a horizontal line across the bottom square. You will be drawing lines between nodes.

28 Save in Sketchbook. Save the project. You've done most of the work of the drawing for this block. But you have done only one quarter of the block. To speed up the rest of the drawing, we are going to Clone and Rotate.

29 Press Ctrl+A to select all of the drawing.

30 Click the black square in the corner of the Select tool button to get the Symmetry menu.

31 Click Clone and then click Rot 90.

EQ4 Magic **57**

32 While the cloned piece is selected, carefully hold and drag it to a position in the middle of the right side of the block. This is what I call "parking." It should fit very neatly on the grid.

33 Click Clone and Rot 90 again and park the selected piece in the middle of the bottom edge of the block.

34 Do this Clone, Rot 90, and park one more time to get all four parts of the star.

35 Save in Sketchbook. Save the project.

36 Click the Color tab and color the block.

37 Click the View Sketchbook button. Click the last drawing of the block. Click Notecard. Type in the name of this block (Feathered Ohio Star) and add any notes you desire. Close the Notecard.

38 Delete any unnecessary blocks from the Sketchbook by clicking the block and clicking the Delete button on the Sketchbook. Close the Sketchbook.

39 Save the project.

40 Add the block to My Libraries. See the instructions on pages 56-57 in the EQ4 Design Cookbook.

41 Save in Sketchbook. Save the project.

 Tips and Tricks:

- If there is any leaking of the color between patches, you did not park your cloned image carefully enough. Back up to one of your saved drawings and try again. Only after you have proven to yourself that your block is perfect should you go back into the Sketchbook and delete unnecessary construction drawings.

- You may use this block in a Horizontal or On-Point quilt layout very effectively.

- You can experiment with other feathered star lessons. See: DRAWING A FEATHERED VARIABLE STAR and DRAWING A FEATHERED 8-POINTED STAR .

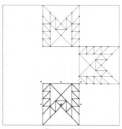

Step 33

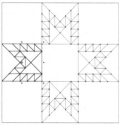

Step 34

Step 36

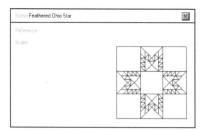

Step 37

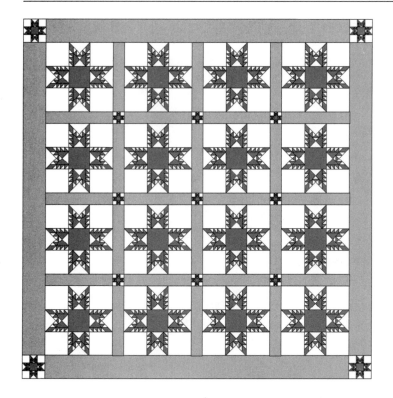

Examples of quilts using the Feathered Ohio Star block

EQ4 Magic 59

Drawing a Feathered Variable Star

It is so much easier to draw a Feathered Star
block in EQ4 than on paper. The design takes
time to create, but it is very rewarding.
The Feathered Variable Star is based on the
4-patch Variable Star block.

4-Patch Variable Star block

1   On the WORKTABLE menu, click Work
    on Block.

2   On the BLOCK menu, point to New Block,
    click EasyDraw.

3   On the BLOCK MENU, click Drawing
    Board Setup.

4   In the box for Snap to Grid Points, Hori-
    zontal divisions, type 42. Press the Tab key
    on your keyboard.

5   In the box for Vertical divisions, type 42.
    Press Tab.

6   In the Block Size, Horizontal, type 21.
    Press Tab.

7   In the Block Size Vertical, type 21. Click
    OK.

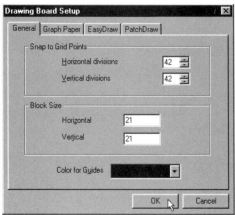

Steps 3-7

8   On the VIEW menu, click Rulers to put a
    check (if there is not a check already).

9   Click the Snap to Grid tool. No other snap-
    to tools should be enabled at this time. See:
    USING ADVANCED DRAWING FEATURES and
    CUSTOMIZING THE DRAWING TOOLBAR.

10 Click the Line tool and draw vertical lines
    from the top of the block to the bottom at
    ruler markings 6½" and 14½".

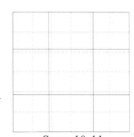

Steps 10-11

11 Draw horizontal lines connecting the left
    and right sides of the block at ruler
    markings 6½" and 14½".

12 Save in Sketchbook. Save the project.

Drawing the area for the "feathers"

13 In the corner squares of the block, draw
    parallel lines one inch to the outside of the
    outline of the star. Cross the lines to form a
    square at the inside point. Note illustration.

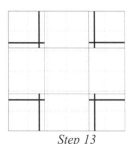

Step 13
(For emphasis, the new lines
have been darkened.)

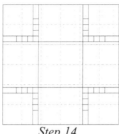

Step 14

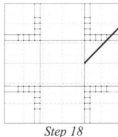

Step 18
(Again, the new line has been
darkened for emphasis.)

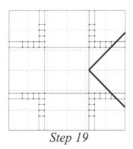

Step 19

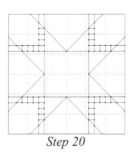

Step 20

14 Draw three 1" squares along each arm of the bands you just drew, as illustrated.

15 Save in Sketchbook. Save the project.

 Tricks:

- Using Ctrl+Z immediately to undo your last drawing line is a quick way to erase mistakes. You may do this up to 10 times successively to erase your last 10 or fewer lines.

- Click the Zoom In tool on the left toolbar and drag a box (marquee) around your drawing area in order to enlarge the area for easier drawing.

- Save in Sketchbook and Save the project often as you construct this block so you have a backup in case of error. You can always delete your construction drawings from the Sketchbook later.

16 Click the dark square in the corner of the Edit tool to get the Edit menu.

17 Click the right vertical line of the center square and click the word "Half" on the Edit menu. A node will appear in the center of this line.

18 Click the Line tool and draw a line from that center node 45 degrees diagonally up and to the right to the edge of the block. If your drawing line is straight rather than jagged as you extend the line, you are right on track. You will be crossing a corner of one of the squares you've just drawn. Be sure to extend this line all the way to the edge of the block.

19 Draw another line from that center node 45 degrees diagonally down and to the right to the edge of the block. Be sure to extend this line all the way to the edge of the block.

20 Repeat the directions for dividing the line in half and for drawing the diagonal lines to form the points of the star with the other three sides of the center square. (Note illustration.)

21 Save in Sketchbook. Save the project.

EQ4 Magic 61

Drawing a Feathered Variable Star

22 You need to draw lines 1" away and parallel to these lines you just drew to get the area for the feathers. The lines will extend from the tip of the diamond forming on the star points to a grid dot on the center square of the block and form a square at the inside junction of the star points. See the illustration. You will have some extra lines forming here that will be deleted later.

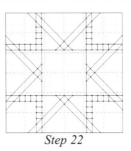

Step 22

Tricks:

• **You may want to use the Zoom In tool on the left toolbar when you draw these lines for visual ease.**

• **On the Rulers, you will see that the lines you're drawing measure to be 1 ½" apart. That's the *diagonal* measurement between these parallel lines at the edge of the block. If you take a right angle (perpendicular) measurement between the parallel lines, you will see that that space is 1" apart.**

Step 23
(Refresh Screen)

23 Save in Sketchbook. Save the project. Click the Refresh Screen button on the left toolbar.

Trick:
The Refresh tool will clean up your drawing board by eliminating ghost or cut-off lines.
You have just defined the areas for the feathers in the centers of all four sides of the star. Notice that the outside line is longer than the inside line. This is important.

Step 24

24 Click the dark square in the corner of the Edit tool to get the Edit menu. Set the Partition number to 5 by clicking the up or down arrow.

25 Click each of the *outside* (longer) lines of the centers of the sides of the star and click Partition to segment these lines into 5 pieces.

26 Click the down arrow to change the Partition setting to 4.

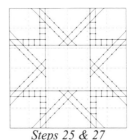

Steps 25 & 27

27 Click each of the *inside* (shorter) lines of the centers of the sides of the star. Click Partition to segment these lines into 4 pieces.

28 Click the Snap to Grid button to disable it.

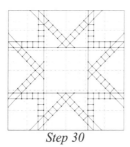

Step 30

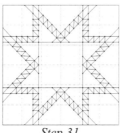

Step 31

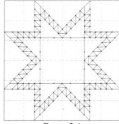

Step 34

Step 35

*A quilt using
the Feathered
Variable Star
block*

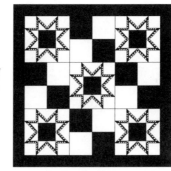

29 Click the Snap to Nodes button to enable it.

30 Click the Line tool and draw lines to connect the nodes on each arm of the star to get a series of squares.

31 Now draw diagonal lines to divide all the squares around the star into half-square triangles. The illustration will help guide you.

32 Save in Sketchbook. Save the project.

33 Your cleanup job is to remove the extraneous lines extending around the diamond points and the center (drawn in step 22). Click the Select tool.

34 To select multiple lines, hold down the Shift key as you click each line. You may want to do this for only two lines at a time at each star point. Press the Delete key on your keyboard. Continue around the star, deleting all extra lines that were used in construction.

35 Click the Color tab and color your block.

36 Click View Sketchbook. Click the Blocks tab. Click the last drawing of the block. Click Notecard. Type in the name of this block (Feathered Variable Star) and add any notes you desire. Close the Notecard by clicking the X.

37 Delete any unnecessary blocks from the Sketchbook. Close the Sketchbook by clicking the X.

38 Save the project.

39 Add the block to My Libraries according to the instructions on pages 56-57 in the EQ4 Design Cookbook.

 Trick:

• **You may use Ctrl+Z to undo a color immediately after you have misplaced it.**

• **You can experiment with other feathered star lessons. See:** DRAWING A FEATHERED OHIO STAR and DRAWING A FEATHERED 8-POINTED STAR .

40 Save in Sketchbook. Save the project.

EQ4 Magic   63

Drawing a Feathered 8-Pointed Star

Drafting this block is not for the beginner. The instructions here take some patience to follow. Read through the steps carefully, follow them exactly, and you should be successful.

1   On the WORKTABLE menu, click Work on Block.

2   On the BLOCK menu, point to New Block, click EasyDraw.

3   On the LIBRARIES menu, click Block Library.

4   In the Block Library, double-click EQ Libraries if this book is not already open. Double-click 1 Classic Pieced.

5   Click Eight-Point Stars. If you have four blocks in your block display, click the Diamond block in the upper-right corner. The name of the block will appear if you hold the cursor over the block for a second without clicking. Click Copy. Click Close.

6   Click View Sketchbook.

7   Click the Blocks tab. Click the Diamond block if it is not already selected.

8   Click Edit to put this block on the EasyDraw drawing board.

9   On the BLOCK menu, click Drawing Board Setup.

10   On the General tab, type 120 for Snap to Grid Points, Horizontal divisions. Press the Tab key on your keyboard.

11   Type 120 for Vertical divisions. Press Tab.

12   Type 15 for Block Size, Horizontal. Press Tab.

13   Type 15 for Block Size, Vertical. Click OK.

14   On the VIEW menu, click Rulers to put a check there (if there is not a check already).

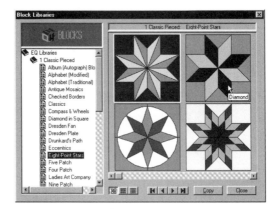

Steps 4-5

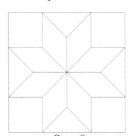

*Step 8
(Diamond block)*

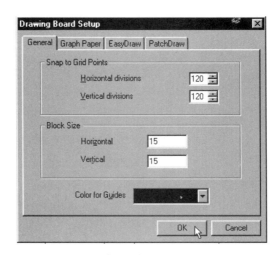

Steps 9-13

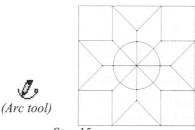

(Arc tool)

Step 15

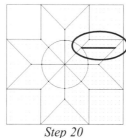

Step 20
(For emphasis, the new line has been darkened and circled.)

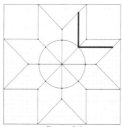

Step 21
(Again, the new lines have been darkened for emphasis.)

15 Click the Arc tool. You will be drawing 4 arcs in the center of the star to make a circle that is 6" in diameter. The ruler markings to connect are:

- Top center 7½" horizontal and 4½" vertical
- Left 7½" vertical and 4½" horizontal
- Bottom 7½" horizontal and 10½" vertical
- Right 10½" horizontal and 7½" vertical

Note:

If your arc is not curving in the direction you want, press the Spacebar on your keyboard before letting go of the drag and the arc will reverse its curve.

16 Save in Sketchbook.

17 On the BLOCK menu, click Drawing Board Setup. You will need your advanced drawing features and a customized drawing board for this drafting. See: USING ADVANCED DRAWING FEATURES and CUSTOMIZING THE DRAWING BOARD. Click the EasyDraw tab.

18 The only snap-to tool selected should be Snap to Grid. In the box for Node Size, click Large. All the nodes where lines cross or join will have larger nodes. Click OK.

19 Click the Line tool.

20 Starting with the node from the arc that crosses the diagonal line in the top-right quadrant of the star, carefully draw a horizontal line that is exactly parallel to the right horizontal arm of the star.

21 Start from the same node and draw a vertical line that is exactly parallel to the right vertical line of the star.

Note:

- You need to try your best to keep these lines smooth. They will be straight, but you can tell you are drawing a good line because it will be smooth without any jags in the line. Do your best to have as few of these jags as possible. Using the Zoom In tool will help you.

EQ4 Magic 65

- **It is all right to extend these lines beyond the edge of the star in order to join with a grid dot. Just be sure the extended line does not connect to the outline of the block. Extended lines ending in open space will be cut off automatically when you Save in Sketchbook.**
- **You may need to disable the Snap-to tools to get lines to go where you want them to be.**

22 Draw diagonal lines parallel to the diagonal lines on the top-center part of the star.

23 Save in Sketchbook. Save the project.

24 Continue drawing these parallel lines around the star. Save in Sketchbook and Save the project after every second star point is complete. The extra drawings can be deleted from the Sketchbook later. Click the Refresh Screen tool.

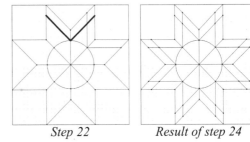

Step 22   *Result of step 24*

When you finish this first set of lines, your drawing should look like the illustration.

 Trick:
Use Ctrl+Z to undo any immediately previous line.

25 You no longer need the center drafting lines, so click the Select tool. Hold down the Shift key and click each of the arc lines to select them. Release the Shift key. Press the Delete key on your keyboard.

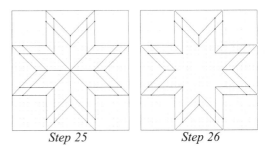

Step 25   *Step 26*

26 Hold down the Shift key again and click each of the lines crisscrossing the center of the star. Release the Shift key. Press the Delete key.

27 You also do not need the lines separating the inside points of the star. These lines kind of look like miter seams for the inside points. Hold down the Shift key and click each of these "mitered seam" lines. Press the Delete key.

Step 27

28 Save in Sketchbook. Save the project. Click the Refresh Screen tool.

29 Click the dark square in the corner of the Edit tool to get the Edit menu.

30 Click the down arrow to set Partition to 3.

Steps 29-30

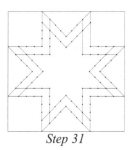

Step 31

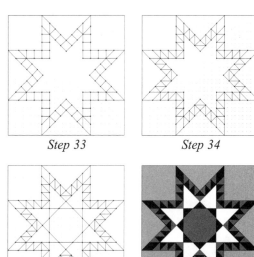

Step 33   *Step 34*

Step 36   *Step 38*

A Variable point quilt layout using the Feathered 8-Pointed Star block

31 Click each of the lines of the star that are not part of the diamond tips and click the word Partition on the Edit menu. You will see three nodes added to each of these lines. Sorry, you cannot multiple select lines and Partition. You will Partition 32 lines in all. Click the Refresh Screen tool.

32 Click the Line tool. Click the Snap to Node tool to engage it and click the Snap to Grid tool to disengage it (if you still have it on).

33 Connect the nodes to create squares in the columns outlining each of the star points. Some lines will appear jagged, but if you follow the illustration your 8-pointed star will work out fine.

34 Divide each of these squares into half-square triangles by adding more lines between nodes. See the illustration as a guide. Remember to use Ctrl+Z to undo immediate past drawn lines if necessary.

35 Save in Sketchbook. Save the project.

36 Lastly, draw two overlapping squares in the center of the star as illustrated.

37 Save in Sketchbook. Save the project.

38 Click the Color tab and color the block. Save in Sketchbook.

39 Click View Sketchbook. Click the last drawing of the block. To see the colored version of your block, click on the right-coloring arrows at the bottom of the Sketchbook. Click Notecard. Type in the name of this block (Feathered 8-Pointed Star) and add any notes you desire. Close the Notecard by clicking the X.

40 Delete any unnecessary blocks from the Sketchbook (see page 80 in the EQ4 Design Cookbook). Close the Sketchbook.

41 Save the project.

42 Add the block to My Libraries according to the instructions on pages 56-57 in the EQ4 Design Cookbook.

Drawing a Feathered 8-Pointed Star

EQ4 Magic 67

Drawing a 45° Diamond Block

1 On the WORKTABLE menu, click Work on Block.

2 On the BLOCK menu, point to New Block, click EasyDraw.

3 On the BLOCK menu, click Drawing Board setup.

4 The General tab should be open and the number for Snap to Grid Points should be highlighted for Horizontal divisions. Type in 48. Press the Tab key to advance to Vertical divisions and type in 48.

5 Press the Tab key to advance to Block size and type in 6 for Horizontal. Press Tab and type in 6 for Vertical. This is just for drawing purposes. You will change this number in Print options when you designate size of the block for a printout.

6 Click the Graph Paper tab. Under Number of Divisions, the number for Horizontal is highlighted. Type in 2. Press the Tab key and type in 2 for Vertical.

7 Click the EasyDraw tab. See: USING ADVANCED DRAWING FEATURES and CUSTOMIZING THE DRAWING TOOLBAR. Under Node Size, click Large. Click OK menu.

8 If the Graph Paper divisions do not show on the worktable, click the Graph Paper tool button.

9 If you do not have Rulers showing on your worktable, click VIEW and click Rulers.

10 Click the Line tool and the Snap to Grid tool. No other snap-to tools should be enabled at this time. Draw these three lines:

    A) A diagonal line from the top left corner to the bottom right corner;

    B) A vertical line from the center of the block to the bottom edge of the block at the 3" mark;

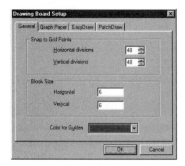

Steps 4-5

Step 6

Step 7

Step 8
(Graph Paper tool)

(sidebar) Drawing a 45° Diamond Block

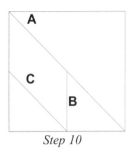

Step 10

Step 11

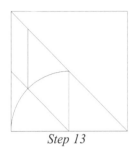

Step 13

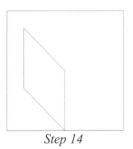

Step 14

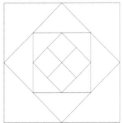

*Monkey Wrench block
(outline and gray scale)*

C) A diagonal line from the center of the bottom edge of the block to the center of the left edge of the block (at the 3" mark for both bottom and side).

11 Click the Arc tool and draw an arc from the center of the block to the bottom left corner of the block.

↳ Note:
If the arc in step 10 isn't curving to the left in a convex curve, press the Spacebar to toggle its position.

12 Save in Sketchbook. Click the Refresh Screen tool button.

↳ Note:
This step of saving in Sketchbook automatically segments the intersecting line.

13 Click the Line tool and the Snap to Node tool. (Click the Snap to Grid tool to deselect it.) Draw a vertical line from the point where the curve intersects the short diagonal line upward to where the line will intersect the long diagonal line. This vertical line will be at the 7/8" mark on the top ruler. Save in Sketchbook to segment lines once again.

14 Click the Select tool. Hold down the Shift key and click all the lines that do not form the diamond. There will be 5 lines in all, including two segments of the arc and three extensions of the diagonal lines of the diamond. Press the Delete key on your keyboard to make them disappear. Presto!

15 Save in Sketchbook. Save the project. Now, you will draw the block into this diamond. You will need to have some knowledge of grid identification for block drafting. Drafting to a diamond is very much like drafting to a square block when you know the grid system.

For an example, let's draw the Monkey Wrench block with this diamond. The Monkey Wrench block can be found in the EQ Libraries, 1 Classic Pieced, and the last block on the Classics page. This specific block is a four-patch block. This means that a graph grid of 4

EQ4 Magic **69**

divides this block into equal segments for drawing the patches. Note that the patches here will all be skewed to the diamond, so you cannot use the square graph paper in EasyDraw. We'll have to draw our own.

Step 16

16 Click the dark square in the corner of the Edit tool. The Edit Arc pop-up menu will appear. In the box next to Partition, use the arrows to get the number 4.

17 Click one of the sides of the diamond. You will see that the Edit Arc pop-up has now changed its title to Edit Line. Click the word Partition. The line will be in 4 evenly spaced sections divided by nodes.

18 Repeat this step for the other three sides of the diamond.

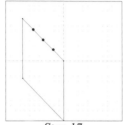 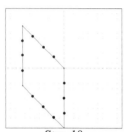

Step 17   *Step 18*
(For emphasis, the new nodes have been darkened)

19 Click the Line tool. Use the nodes to draw your "graph paper" dividing the diamond. ***Do not save in Sketchbook*** at this time.

20 Click the Select tool. Hold down the Shift key and click each of the "graph paper" lines (6 lines in total). Release the mouse.

21 On the BLOCK menu, click Convert to Guides. Your "graph paper" lines will now show as faded dotted lines that will be your drawing guides.

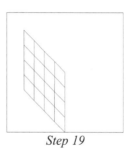

Step 19

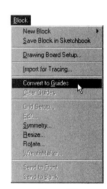

Step 21

22 Click the Line tool. Draw the largest triangles of the Monkey Wrench block by drawing lines connecting the centers of all four sides. (You will make a rectangle.)

23 Click the dark square in the corner of the Edit tool to get the pop-up menu. Click one of the lines you just drew. Click the word Half to get a node segmenting that line in the middle.

24 Repeat step 23 for the other three lines.

25 Click the Line tool. Draw lines connecting these new nodes and form a diamond in the block. Click Refresh Screen.

Step 22   *Step 25*

Step 26

Step 27

26 Repeat steps 23-25 (you will form another rectangle instead of a diamond). You are working your way into the center of the block.

27 Repeat steps 23-24 one more time. Click the Line tool. This time you will be connecting opposite nodes to form a four-patch in the center (the checkerboard). Click the Color tab and color the block.

28 Save in Sketchbook. Save the project. This block, and specifically this lesson, can be used to get accurate templates for the diamond blocks in the SKEWING TO A DIAMOND LAYOUT. The size of the corner squares of your Diamond quilt will be half the size of the block you need to print out. For example, if a corner square from the Diamond quilt measures 28 inches finished, the size of the block for this diamond template printout would have to be 56 inches.

EQ4 Magic   71

Drawing a 45° Diamond Block

Making a Transparent Color Effect

With the expanded color palette, it is easier to find colors to coordinate for a transparent color effect.

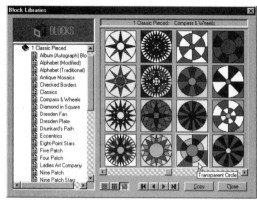

Steps 2-4

1   Click LIBRARIES and Block Library.

2   Double-click EQ Libraries if the book isn't already open. Double-click 1 Classic Pieced.

3   Click Compass & Wheels.

4   Click the 16 block display button at the bottom center of the menu. The Transparent Circle block is in the bottom row, second from the right. Rest your cursor over the block without clicking and the name of the block will appear. Click the block and click Copy. Close the Library.

5   Click View Sketchbook. Click the Blocks tab. Click the Transparent Circle block and click Edit.

6   Click the Color tab.

7   Right-click on any solid color on the Fabrics & Colors palette. On the pop-up menu, click Show 4 rows and 32 color chips will be displayed at one time.

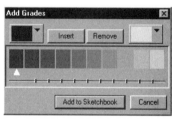

Step 8

8   Click the first red chip in the top-left corner. Right-click to get the pop-up menu. Click Add Grades.

You will see a display with 10 colors grading between red and yellow. For this demonstration, we don't need 10 colors.

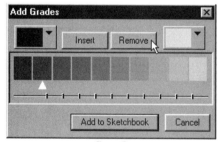

Step 9

9   Position your cursor on the first chip to the right of the red at the left end. Click the chip. Click Remove three times.

10 Position your cursor on the third chip to the left of the yellow chip at the right end. Click the chip. Click Remove three times. The cursor will jump to the next chip on the right so be sure you do not delete the yellow accidentally or you will have to start over.

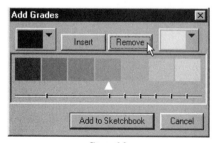

Step 10

Step 14
(Note how the new colors appear at the end of the palette)

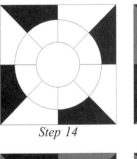

Step 14

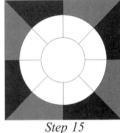

Step 15

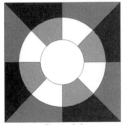

Step 16

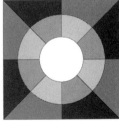

Step 17

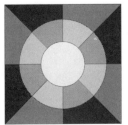

Step 18

11 Click Add to Sketchbook. These four color gradations will be at the end of your palette display.

12 Click the bright blue chip at the bottom of the 6th column from the left of the color palette display. Right-click and click Add Grades.

13 You will see 10 colors grading between blue and yellow. Repeat steps 9 and 10 to reduce the number of chips to 4. Click Add to Sketchbook.

A transparency effect happens when there appears to be an overlapping of patches and the overlapping patches are colored with a hue that is a probable blend of the colors on either side. For example, if you position a blue patch on one side and a yellow patch on the other side, the patch in the middle could be colored green to get the effect that the yellow and blue blended in the middle patch.

Follow these steps to color this block with a transparency effect.

14 Scroll to the end of your color palette. Click the red that you used to get graded colors. Click every other outside shape in the block to color it red.

15 Click the blue and color the other alternate shapes.

16 Click one of the middle graded colors between the red and yellow and color the patches next to the red patches.

17 Click one of the middle graded colors between the blue and yellow and color the patches next to the blue patches.

18 Click the yellow and color the center. Save in Sketchbook. Save the project.

Do you get the feeling that the circle is yellow and is transparent?

Setting a Quilt with Transparency

1 On the WORKTABLE menu, click Work on Quilt.

EQ4 Magic 73

2 On the QUILT menu, point to New quilt, click Horizontal.

3 Click the Layout tab and make these adjustments:

- Number of blocks: 4 Horizontal and Vertical
- Size of blocks: 12 Width and Height
- Sashing: 2.00 Width and Height
- Click to check Sash border

4 Click the Layer 1 tab.

5 Click the Set tool. Click the Transparent Circle block in the Sketchbook Blocks display if it isn't already selected.

6 Position your cursor on a block and Ctrl+click to set all the blocks at once.

7 Click Libraries and click Block Library.

8 Open the EQ Library and double-click 1 Classic Pieced. Click Striped Borders. You will have to use the arrow to scroll down to find this in the alphabetical listing.

9 Click the 9-block display button. The Stripe 5 block is in the lower right corner. Rest your cursor over the block without clicking to confirm the name. Click the block to select and click Copy. Close the Library.

10 Click the Stripe 5 block in the Sketchbook Blocks display. It's okay to use the colored version of this block for now. Position your cursor on one of the horizontal sashes and Ctrl+click.

11 Position your cursor on one of the vertical sashes and Ctrl+click.

12 Click the Rotate tool on the right toolbar. Position your cursor on one of the horizontal sashes and Ctrl+click.

We're going to color the pieced sashing with some transparency, too. We want a blending color between the red and the blue this time. Actually, for some contrast, we are going to look for one blending color that favors the red and one that favors the blue.

Making a Transparent Color Effect

Step 3

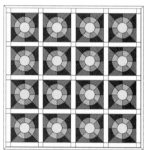

Steps 5-6

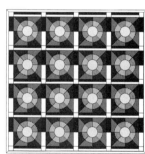

Steps 10-11

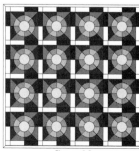

Step 12

(Click and drag this bar if you want to move the Add Grades menu)

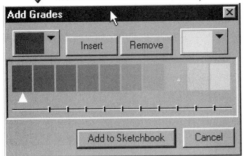

Steps 13-14

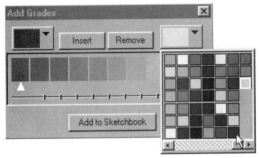

Step 15

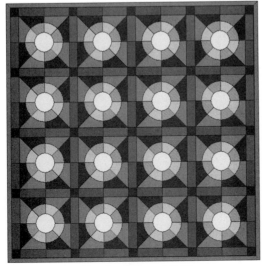

Result of steps 17-19

13 Click the Paintbrush tool. Click the red chip at the end of the palette display that you used to color the block. If you have lost track of where it is, click the Spraycan tool on the right toolbar. Put your cursor on one of the red patches and click. The red will immediately show on the color palette. Click the Paintbrush tool again.

14 Right-click on the selected red chip. Click Add Grades. The menu may be crowded to one side of your worktable, so put your cursor on the top bar of the menu and drag it toward the center of the worktable.

15 The menu shows possibilities for grading between red and yellow, but we want to grade between red and blue. Click the arrow next to the yellow chip. The whole color palette pops up. Scroll to the end of the palette to find the blue you used to color the block. (Sorry, you can't use the Spraycan tool here to help.) Click the blue color chip.

16 Click Insert and you will see graded color chips between red and blue. You may remove all but four of these chips in this gradation. Keep the end chips and choose one of the center chips that favors red but has a blue influence and one that favors blue but has a red influence. Remove the rest. Click Add to Sketchbook.

17 Click the "red with a blue influence" chip, position your cursor on the white patch of the horizontal pieced sashing, and Ctrl+click. Repeat for the same patch of the vertical pieced sashing.

18 Click the "blue with a red influence" chip, position your cursor on the blue patch of the horizontal pieced sashing, and Ctrl+click. Repeat for the vertical pieces.

19 I used the red for the Corner stones and blue for the narrow border. Set with Ctrl+click.

20 Save in Sketchbook. Save the project.

EQ4 Magic 75

Making a Transparent Color Effect

Expanding the Color Palette

With "Bibbity-bobbity-boo" and a click of the mouse button, you can change those line drawings into instant color! Following the installation of the CD ROM that came with this book, you can enhance the color palette in EQ4 with more colors. And you can get a lesson in color, besides. The notes in Help relating to color actually include a brief explanation of Faber Birren's "modern" theories of color harmony. Be sure to check out "About EQ4 Colors" on the Help menu.

Look at every Help message relating to Color. The information is most helpful and won't be repeated here as long as I can tell you where to find the resource easily.

Start experimenting and exploring the EQ4 color palette with a new project file. You don't have to have a drawing, a block, or a quilt in the Sketchbook in order to do this. In fact, it may be better if you don't. You could decide to set up different color palette possibilities and save the blank file under different names for each palette. You could use that color file for a project later and save it under a different name in order to keep the color palette intact for another use.

Don't be afraid to lose the original default EQ4 palette that you've been used to. To restore the EQ4 color palette:

1 Right-click the color palette.

2 Click Customize Palette.

3 Under Change, click Change palette.

4 In the next box, click the arrow to get EQ4 default palette.

5 Click OK.

That's just to give you a safety net before you start experimenting, in case you worry about getting back to where you started. Surfing the expanded color palette possibilities may be as addicting as surfing the web. One thing can lead to another.

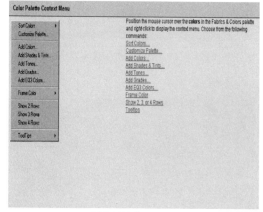

EQ4 Help Menu

Step 2

Step 3

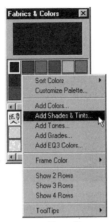

Step 2

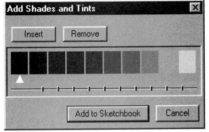

Step 3

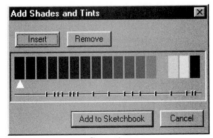

Step 4

Step 5

Follow these steps to start your exploration of the color world in EQ4.

1   Click the Paintbrush tool on the quilt worktable or the block coloring worktable and you will see the Fabrics & Colors palette.

2   Position your cursor on your favorite color in the color palette, click to select and then right-click.

The pop-up menu will show you several options for adding to and customizing your color palette. You can choose to add colors and sort them. You can also add "Shades & Tints," "Tones," and "Grades," among other things.

3   Click Add Shades & Tints.

Your selected color from the original color palette is in the center of the line of 10 shades and tints. "Shades" are the color (or hue) with some black added, and they are graded to the left of the color. "Tints" are the color with some white added, and they are graded to the right of the color. To many of us, these are called "pastels."

4   You may add to this line-up of shades and tints by clicking any of the color patches. You will see the white arrow point to that patch. Click Insert and a color patch will be added to the spectrum. You may add more patches between various shades and tints until you get a maximum of 16 colors in this line. You may hear a chime to tell you when you've started to get greedy. There will also be a black rectangle at the right end of the line when there's enough.

5   Click Add to Sketchbook.

You will find these new colors at the end of your palette display.

Adding tones works similarly. When you select a color, right-click and select Add Tones, you will see a display with your color on the right and grayed and lightened values to the left. In order to get Tones, color plus white and black (gray) are combined. You can use the Insert tool to get up to 16 grayed gradations of a color.

EQ4 Magic   77

Tips and Tricks:

- Complete a lesson of how to use gradations between two hues. See: MAKING A TRANSPARENT COLOR EFFECT.

- Be sure to consult the Help notes in EQ4 for ways to add custom colors and to optimize colors from added fabrics.

COLORING A BLOCK WITH SHADES AND TINTS

(This can also be done with Tones and Grades.)

1 In LIBRARIES, click Block Library. Double-click EQ Libraries if it isn't open. Double-click 1 Classic Pieced. Click Dresden Plate.

2 Click the 16-block display button. Look for the block named "8 Petal Small Center Dresden Plate." It's the second block down on the far right column. Hold your cursor on the block, without clicking, to confirm the name. Then click the block and click Copy. Click Close.

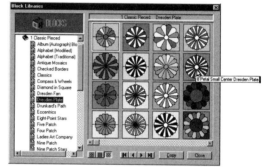

Step 2

3 Click View Sketchbook. Click the Blocks tab. Click the "8 Petal" block.

4 Click the far left arrow key to get the line drawing of that block. Click Edit.

5 With the block on the EasyDraw work-table, click the Color tab.

Using the new shades and tints you just made, you will color the block. There are 32 petals on this Dresden plate, so you will be able to use each of the 16 shades and tints twice.

Step 5

10 Scroll to the right end of the color palette to view the 16 shades and tints you just added. Click the darkest chip of the set. Click two opposite petals on the Dresden plate to color.

11 Click the next slightly lighter chip in the series. Click opposite petals next to the first two you just colored.

12 Continue around the plate so the colors become successively lighter until all are colored.

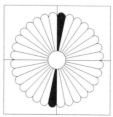

Step 10

Step 11

Expanding the Color Palette

Step 13

You will see that two opposite quarters of the Dresden plate are on the light side and two are on the dark side.

13 Color the background dark behind the light quarters and light behind the dark quarters. Color the center anything you like.

14 Save in Sketchbook. Save the project.

Tips and Tricks:

- Be aware that you cannot save this block to My Library and have the colors transfer to another file. That's because these colors are not in the My Library palette.

- In the EQ Libraries, there are many blocks that accommodate a shade/tint/tone gradation. Look in 1 Classic Pieced, Classics, and find Double Wedding Ring, Log Cabin, Lady of the Lake, Flying Geese, Monkey Wrench, and Bear's Paw, to name some to get you started. Go into 1 Classic Pieced, Compass and Wheels and see many more blocks. Then 1 Classic Pieced, Dresden Fans and 1 Classic Pieced, Dresden Plates will add to your list of possibilities.

EQ4 Magic **79**

Adding Text to an Exported Snapshot

Using Word 97 or 2000 you can add text directly onto an Exported Snapshot from EQ4.

Create a copy of an exported snapshot

1 Have a colored block or quilt on the worktable.

2 Click the Export Snapshot button on the left toolbar.

3 A crosshair cursor will appear. Position the cursor at the top left corner of the block or quilt and carefully drag the cursor so the select box outlines the block/quilt and includes nothing else on the drawing board

4 Let go of your cursor and click Copy to Windows clipboard on the Export Snapshot menu. (You will not see anything happen, but the snapshot will be on the clipboard.)

Tricks:

• If you make a mistake when you are creating the Snapshot, close the Export Snapshot menu by clicking the X and repeat steps 2-4.

• You may also click to Save as bitmap file from the Export Snapshot menu. I like to save my bitmaps in a folder of their own in EQ4. If EQ4 does not appear in the Save in dialog box, click the down arrow and navigate to find where you saved EQ4. Click the Create New Folder button and type EQ4 Bitmaps. Double-click this new folder (it will appear in the Save in dialog box). Place your cursor in the Filename dialog box, click, and type in a new name for your bitmap. Click Save.

Now we're ready to **open a Word document** so we can add text to your snapshot.

1 In a New Word Document, press Ctrl+V (or click EDIT, Paste). Your bitmap will magically appear.

2 To resize the image, click the picture. On the FORMAT menu, click Picture to get the pop-out menu.

3 Click the Size tab and use the arrows to size the picture (we made ours 5x5). (The picture will automatically resize proportionately.) Click OK.

Step 1

Step 2
(Export Snapshot tool)

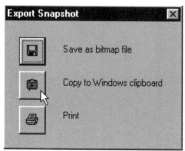

Step 4

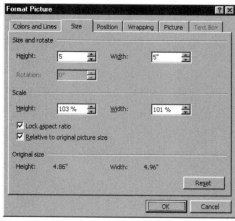

Step 3

Step 4

Step 5

Steps 6-7

Step 9

☀ **Trick:**
If you want to stretch out the picture to fill your rectangular page, uncheck the boxes for Lock aspect ratio and Relative to original picture size.

4 Click INSERT, Text Box. Click, hold, and drag a box on top of the image. Release the mouse and a box will appear.

5 Type in the text. (You may type a single letter or an entire paragraph.)

☀ **Trick:**
If you are familiar with Word, feel free to experiment with the fonts, size, and alignment of your text.

6 The outline of the text box is selected and you may adjust the size of the text box to fit closely around the text. Hold your cursor over one of the white square nodes on the box outline. When the cursor is a double-headed arrow, click, hold, and drag the box to change it to the size you desire.

7 On the FORMAT menu, click Text Box, Colors and Lines tab. For Fill, Color, click the arrow and click No Fill. For Line, Color, click the arrow and click No Line. Click OK.

8 To move the text box and text, position your cursor on the edge of the text box until you get the cross arrow cursor. Click, hold, and drag your text box to the desired position.

9 Repeat steps 4-8 for each text box to be included on the picture.

10 Save your document.

☀ **Tips and Tricks:**
- **You can include your picture with text in a handout. See:** MAKING A PROFESSIONAL-LOOKING HANDOUT.
- **You can add text to a metafile. See:** ADDING TEXT TO A METAFILE.

Adding Text to an Exported Snapshot

EQ4 Magic **81**

Adding Text to a Metafile

Using Word 97 or 2000 you can add text directly onto a Metafile from EQ4.

Create a copy of a metafile

1 Have a block on the drawing worktable.

Tip:
The Export Metafile tool produces line drawings of blocks (even if you have a colored block on the worktable when you use the tool).

2 Click the Export Metafile button on the left toolbar.

3 On the Export Metafile menu press the Delete key on your keyboard, type 5 for Width, press the Tab key, and type 5 for Height.

4 Click Copy to Windows clipboard. (You will not see anything happen, but the metafile will be on the clipboard.)

Trick:
You may also click to Save as Windows metafile from the Export Metafile menu. I like to save my metafiles in a folder of their own in EQ4. If EQ4 does not appear in the Save in dialog box, click the down arrow and navigate to find where you saved EQ4. Click the Create New Folder button and type EQ4 Metafiles. Double-click the new folder (it will appear in the Save in dialog box). Place your cursor in the Filename dialog box, click, and type in a new name for your metafile. Click Save.

Now we're ready to **open a Word document** so we can add text to your metafile.

1 In a New Word Document, press Ctrl+V (or click EDIT, Paste). Your metafile will magically appear.

Trick:
If you don't like the size you selected for the metafile you can resize the image. Click the picture. On the FORMAT menu, click Picture, and click the Size tab. Use the arrows to size the picture (it will automatically resize proportionately). If you want to stretch out the picture to fill your rectangular page, uncheck the boxes for Lock aspect ratio and Relative to original picture size.

Step 1

Step 2
(Export Metafile tool)

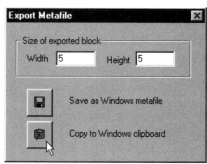
Step 4

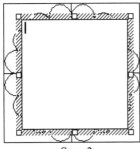

Step 2

Step 3

Steps 4-5

Step 7

2 Click INSERT, Text Box. Click, hold, and drag a box on top of the image. Release the mouse and a box will appear.

3 Type in the text. (You may type a single letter or an entire paragraph.)

Trick:
If you are familiar with Word, feel free to experiment with the fonts, size, and alignment of your text.

4 The outline of the text box is selected and you may adjust the size of the text box to fit closely around the text. Hold your cursor over one of the white square nodes on the box outline. When the cursor is a double-headed arrow, click, hold, and drag the box to change it to the size you desire.

5 On the FORMAT menu, click Text Box, Colors and Lines tab. For Fill, Color, click the arrow and click No Fill. For Line, Color, click the arrow and click No Line. Click OK.

6 To move the text box and text, position your cursor on the edge of the text box until you get the cross arrow cursor. Click, hold, and drag your text box to the desired position.

7 Repeat steps 2-6 for each text box to be included on the picture.

8 Save your document.

Tips and Tricks:

- **You can include your picture with text in a handout. See:** MAKING A PROFESSIONAL-LOOKING HANDOUT.

- **You can add text to a colored block or a quilt (an export snapshot). See:** ADDING TEXT TO AN EXPORTED SNAPSHOT.

EQ4 Magic **83**

Adding Text to a Metafile

Making a Star Sash Quilt

In this lesson, we're going to create a quilt with star sashing. For this quilt, we are going to draw our own blocks. This will help to understand the size proportion of the sashing and the blocks. After making this quilt, you can experiment to design your own. Before starting, you must always know two things: the size of the blocks and the size of the sashing (these two items must be in proportion to each other). Let's begin by drawing the two blocks.

Block 1 - Sash block

1   On the WORKTABLE menu, click Work on Block.

2   On the BLOCK menu, point to New Block, click EasyDraw.

3   On the BLOCK menu, click Drawing Board Setup.

4   For the Snap to Grid Points, type in 18 for Horizontal divisions. Press the Tab key on the keyboard. Type in 6 for Vertical. Press Tab.

5   Type in 9 for Block Size Horizontal. Press Tab. Type in 9 for Vertical.

6   Click the Graph Paper tab.

7   For the Number of Divisions, type 2 for Horizontal. Press Tab. Type 2 for Vertical.

8   Under Options, click the down arrow by the Style box. Click Graph paper lines. Click OK.

9   Make sure the Snap to Grid tool is selected. Do not enable other snap-to buttons at this time. See: USING ADVANCED DRAWING TOOLS and CUSTOMIZING THE DRAWING TOOLBARS.

10   Click the Line tool.

↳ Note:
If you don't see the rulers to the left and across the top of your document screen, click VIEW and Ruler.

Step 2

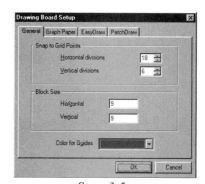

Steps 3-5

Steps 6-8

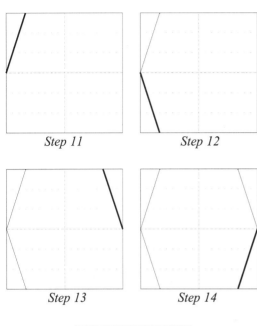

Step 11   *Step 12*

Step 13   *Step 14*

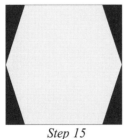

Step 15

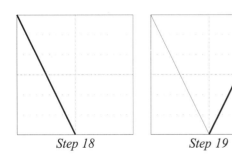

Step 18   *Step 19*

Step 20

11 Draw a diagonal line starting from the 1½" marking on the top ruler down-left to the 4½" marking on the left ruler.

12 Starting at the 4½" marking on the left ruler, draw a diagonal line to the bottom of the block so it is lined up with the 1½" marking on the top ruler.

13 Draw a third diagonal line starting from the 7½" marking on the top ruler down and to the right side of the block so it is lined up with the 4½" marking on the left ruler.

14 Starting at the right edge of the block at the 4½" marking, draw a diagonal line to the bottom of the block so it is lined up with the 7½" marking on the top ruler.

Trick:
You also could have pressed Ctrl+A to select both lines (from steps 11-12), used the Symmetry menu, Clone, and Flip H to create the lines in steps 13-14.

15 Click the Color tab. Color the block. (For this example, I made the edges dark and the center light. You will need to use these colors for the next block so the star points are the same color.)

16 Click Save in Sketchbook. Save the project.

Block 2 - Border block

17 On the BLOCK menu, point to New Block, click EasyDraw.

18 Draw a diagonal line starting from the top-left corner down to the bottom of the block so it is lined up with the 4½" marking on the top ruler.

19 Draw another diagonal line starting from the top-right corner of the block down to the bottom of the block so it is also lined up with the 4½" marking on the top ruler.

20 Click the Color tab. Color the block. (I used the dark color from Step 15 for the two small triangles and the light color for the large-center triangle.)

EQ4 Magic   **85**

Making a Star Sash Quilt

21 Click Save in Sketchbook. Save the project.

22 On the WORKTABLE menu, click Work on Quilt.

23 On the QUILT menu, point to New Quilt, click Horizontal.

Step 23

24 Click the Layout tab. Under Number of Blocks, click the up or down arrows to get 3 for Horizontal. Press the Tab key on your keyboard.

25 Type 3 for Vertical. Press Tab.

26 For Size of blocks, type 9.00 for Width. Press Tab twice.

27 Type 9.00 for Height. Press Tab twice.

28 Type 3.00 for Sashing Width. Press Tab twice.

29 Type 3.00 for Sashing Height.

30 Click Sash border (so there is a check).

31 Click the Borders tab.

32 Click the down arrow by the Style box. Click Corner Blocks.

33 Make each border side 1.5 in size.

34 Click the Layer 1 tab.

35 Click the Set tool.

36 Click the Sash block (Block 1). Find the colored version by clicking the right-arrow button.

37 Position your cursor on a horizontal sashing strip and Ctrl+click. Do the same on a vertical sashing strip.

38 Click the Rotate tool. Position your cursor on a vertical sashing strip. Ctrl+click to rotate all the vertical sashing blocks simultaneously.

Setting the Border Sash Blocks

1 Click the Layer 2 tab.

2 Click the Set tool.

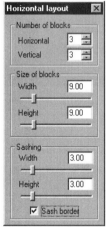

Steps 24-30

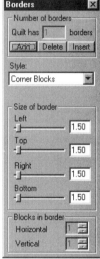

Steps 31-33

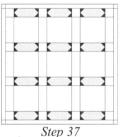

Step 37 (horizontal sash)

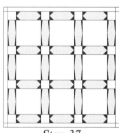

Step 37 (vertical sash)

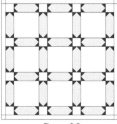

Step 38

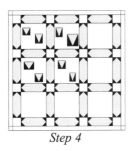

Step 4

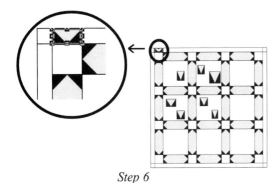

Step 6

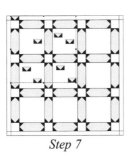

Step 7

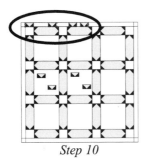

Step 10

3 Click the Border block (Block 2). Find the colored version by clicking the right-arrow button.

4 Click, hold, and drag 8 blocks anywhere on the quilt layout (it will be easier to see them if you set them in blank areas).

📌 **Note:**
If you do not have the Graph Pad on your quilt layout screen, click VIEW and click Graph Pad. You want to have a check mark next to Graph Pad on the menu.

5 Click the Adjust tool. Click one of the blocks you just set.

6 On the Graph Pad, make the following adjustments:

- Horizontal location (top box on far left of Graph Pad): 0.00

- Vertical location (bottom box on far left of Graph Pad): -1.50

- Size width (top box in center of Graph Pad): 3.00

- Size height (bottom box in center of Graph Pad): 1.50

7 With the sized block still selected, hold down the Shift key on your keyboard and click the other 7 blocks. Release the Shift key. Click the Same Size button on the Graph Pad.

8 Click in a free space on the worktable away from the blocks to clear the cursor.

9 Click the block from step 6. Hold down the Shift key and click three other blocks. Release the Shift key.

10 On the Graph Pad, click the Align button with the horizontal line over two squares. This will bring all the selected blocks into alignment with the top of the first block selected. (The Vertical locator box will read -1.50 for each of these blocks.) Clear the cursor.

EQ4 Magic 87

You now need to select and align each block horizontally with the position locator on the left side of the Graph Pad.

11 As you select each of the three blocks in the top row, the upper box number (horizontal) from left to right should be: 12.00, 24.00, and 36.00.

12 Click one of the four remaining unpositioned blocks you set in step 4.

13 Make these location adjustments of the Graph Pad:

- Horizontal location: 0.00

- Vertical location: 39.00

14 With this block selected, hold down the Shift key and click the other three unpositioned blocks. Release the Shift key.

15 On the Graph Pad, click the Align button with the horizontal line over two squares. This will bring all the selected blocks into alighnment with the top of the first block selected. (The Vertical locator box will read 39.00 for each of these blocks.) Clear the cursor.

16 Use the blocks from Step 11 to horizontally set the blocks from step 15. Holding down the Shift key, click on a block from step 11 and click one block from step 15. Release the Shift key. On the Graph Pad, click the Align button with the vertical line to the left of two squares. Repeat this for the other two blocks.

17 Click the Rotate tool.

18 Click each border block at the bottom of the quilt twice.

19 Save in Sketchbook. Save the project.

20 Click the Set tool.

21 With the Border block still selected, click, hold, and drag 8 more blocks anywhere on the quilt layout.

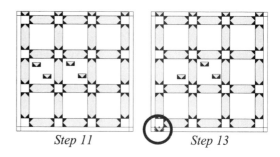

Step 11 *Step 13*

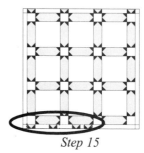

Step 15

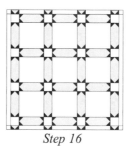

Step 16

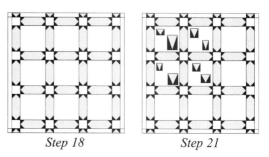

Step 18 *Step 21*

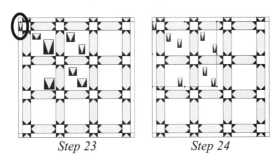

Step 23   *Step 24*

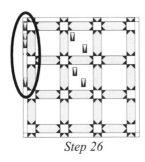

Step 26

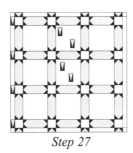

Step 27

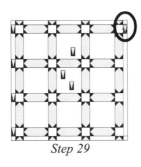

Step 29

22 Click the Adjust tool. Click one of the blocks you just set.

23 On the Graph Pad, make the following adjustments:

- Horizontal location: -1.50
- Vertical location: 0.00
- Size width: 1.50
- Size height: 3.00

24 With the sized block still selected, hold down the Shift key on your keyboard and click the other 7 blocks. Release the Shift key. Click the Same Size button on the Graph Pad. Clear the cursor.

25 Click the block from step 23. Hold down the Shift key and click three other blocks. Release the Shift key.

26 On the Graph Pad, click the Align button with the vertical line to the left of two squares. This will bring all the selected blocks into alignment with the left side of the first block selected. (The Horizontal locator box will read -1.50 for each of these blocks.) Clear the cursor.

You now need to select and align each block vertically with the position locator on the left side of the Graph Pad.

27 As you select each of the three border blocks in the left column, the lower-box number (vertical) from top to bottom should be: 12.00, 24.00, and 36.00.

28 Click one of the four remaining unpositioned blocks you set in step 21.

29 Make these location adjustments of the Graph Pad:

- Horizontal location: 39.00
- Vertical location: 0.00

30 With this block selected, hold down the Shift key and click the other three unpositioned blocks. Release the Shift key.

EQ4 Magic **89**

31 On the Graph Pad, click the Align button with the vertical line to the left of two squares. This will bring all the selected blocks into alignment with the left side of the first block selected. (The Horizontal locator box will read 39.00 for each of these blocks.) Clear the cursor.

32 Use the blocks from Step 27 to vertically set the blocks from step 31. Holding down the Shift key, click on a block from step 27 and click one block from step 31. Release the Shift key. On the Graph Pad, click the Align button with the horizontal line over the two squares. Repeat this for the other two blocks.

33 Click the Rotate tool.

34 Click each border block on the left side of the quilt three times and each border block on the right side of the quilt once.

35 Save in Sketchbook. Save the project.

Tips and Tricks:

- I used the Variable Star block from the EQ Library, 1 Classic Pieced, Nine Patch Stars, for the blocks in Layer 1. You can set other blocks or leave them plain. I also colored the sash center the same dark color as the star points to make them stand out.

- You can use flying geese blocks in the sash. See: SETTING FLYING GEESE IN THE SASHING.

- How you color this quilt can vary the look drastically.

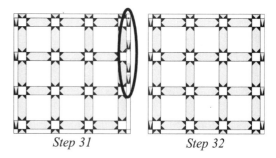

Step 31   *Step 32*

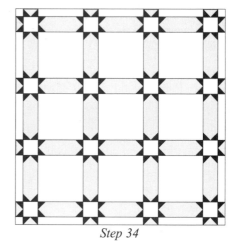

Step 34

Seeing Stars

Chapter 4
Advanced

Chapter 4
Advanced

Making a Professional Handout

Teachers will love a new feature for EQ4 that is included on the CD with this book. After installing the CD, you have the ability to create a metafile in EQ4 that enables you to display a block exploded into construction units. Pairing a metafile and a bitmap of a block drawn in EQ4, printouts for foundation piecing, and templates for traditional piecing for a block will allow teachers to make quality handouts.

🖈 **Note:**
> Directions given here are for MicroSoft® Word 97 and 2000. These programs will accept the .EMF file name extension created for a metafile in EQ4. Please be aware that not all drawing programs will accept the .EMF style. The more current and sophisticated drawing and word processor programs have the ability to accept an .EMF file.

My example for a teaching handout is for what I call an "Interwoven Star" in order to differentiate it from the "Starry Path" block in the EQ4 Library. Here is how I made some changes:

1   In a New Project file, click LIBRARIES, click Block Library.

2   Double-click EQ Libraries if it is not already open and double-click 1 Classic Pieced.

3   Click Old Favorites.

🎩 **Trick:**
> The categories are in alphabetical order, so you may have to scroll down by clicking the down arrow to see this category.

4   Click the 9-block display button at the bottom-center of the Block Library.

5   "Starry Path" is the upper-right block. If you rest your cursor for a second over the block without clicking, the name should appear. Click the block to select it.

6   Click Copy. Click Close.

7   Click View Sketchbook, click the Blocks tab, and click the Starry Path block.

Steps 1-5

Starry Path block

EQ4 Magic 93

8 Click Edit.

Note:
The only snap-to tool that should be enabled is Snap to Grid.

9 Click the Edit tool and click the line ending with A, as shown in the illustration. Drag the line to meet point B.

10 Click the line ending with point C. Drag the line to meet point D.

11 Click the line ending with point E. Drag the line to meet point F.

12 Click the line ending with point G. Drag the line to meet point H.

14 Save in Sketchbook. Save the project.

15 Click on the Select tool. Holding down the Shift key, click the new lines that are now between points A and B, C and D, E and F, and G and H.

16 Press the Delete key on your keyboard to get rid of these extra lines.

17 Save in Sketchbook.

18 Click View Sketchbook, the Blocks tab, and the new block. Click Notecard.

19 Name the block "Interwoven Star." Click the X to close the Notecard.

20 Click the block you just made a notecard for to see its name at the bottom of the Sketchbook.

21 Click the X to close the Sketchbook.

22 Click the Color tab and color the block in grays to go with the illustration of the block on the example handout.

23 Save in Sketchbook. Save project.

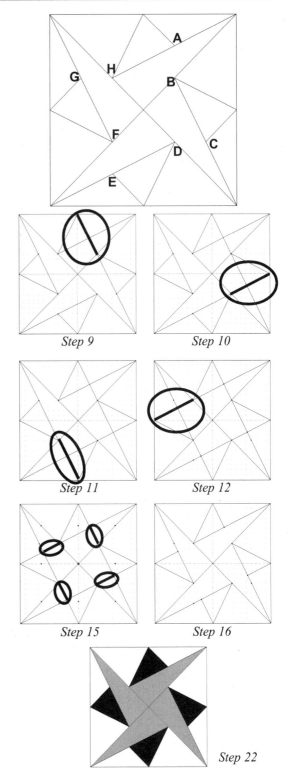

Step 9

Step 10

Step 11

Step 12

Step 15

Step 16

Step 22

Step 2
(Export Snapshot tool)

Step 3

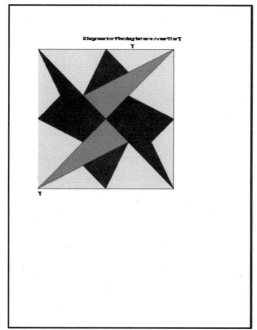

Steps 6-8

Now we're ready to **construct the handout**.

Create a copy of an exported snapshot

1   Click the Export Snapshot button on the left toolbar.

2   A crosshair cursor will appear. Position the cursor at the top left corner of the colored Interwoven Star block and carefully click, hold, and drag the cursor so the select box outlines the block and includes nothing else on the drawing board

3   Let go of your cursor and click Copy to Windows clipboard on the Export Snapshot menu. (You will not see anything happen, but the snapshot will be on the clipboard.)

 Tricks:

*   If you make a mistake when you are creating the Snapshot, close the Export Snapshot menu by clicking the X and repeat steps 1-3.
*   You may also click to Save as bitmap file from the Export Snapshot menu. I like to save my bitmaps in a folder of their own in EQ4. If EQ4 does not appear in the Save in dialog box, click the down arrow and navigate to find where you saved EQ4. Click the Create New Folder button and type EQ4 Bitmaps. Double-click this new folder (it will appear in the Save in dialog box). Place your cursor in the Filename dialog box, click, and type in a new name for your bitmap. Click Save.

4   Open up a New Word Document (Windows 97 or 2000).

 Trick:
You do not have to close EQ4. You can minimize the program by clicking the box in the upper-right corner with the underscore. To maximize the program, click the box in the same corner with the two overlapping boxes.

5   Click FILE and Page Setup. Make the margin settings 1" for all sides (on the Margins tab) and the paper size 8.5" x 11" (on the Paper Size tab). Click OK.

6   Type in the title for your handout.

 Trick:
If you are familiar with Word, feel free to experiment with the fonts, size, and alignment of your title.

EQ4 Magic   95

7 Press Enter two times. (If you centered your title, make sure your text is aligned left.)

8 Press Ctrl+V and the bitmap drawing of your colored block will appear.

9 The bitmap is probably much larger than you want it to be, so click the drawing to select it. Position your cursor over the white node at the bottom- right corner of the block until the double-ended arrow cursor appears. You can now click, hold, and drag the block corner upward diagonally to the left until it is the size you want, approximately 1½" square. The left edge of the block should be even with the left margin of your page.

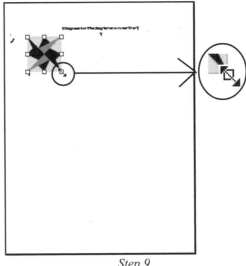

Step 9

10 With the block still selected, click FORMAT, Picture.

Here the directions for Word 97 are different from Word 2000.

In Word 97:

A Click the Position tab. Click the box next to Float over text (so there's a check).

B Click the Wrapping tab. Under Wrapping Style, click Square and under Wrap to, click Right. Click OK.

In Word 2000:

A Click the Layout tab and click the Advanced button to get to the next menu.

B Under Wrapping Style, click Square. Under Wrap text click Right only. Click OK. Click OK again.

11 Position your cursor to the right of the picture and click. Type identification text about the block, and the text will appear only to the right of the block and under it. Press Enter twice at the end of the text.

12 Save the file.

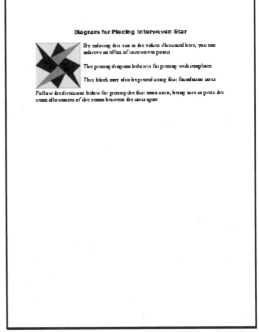

Step 11

Step 14
(Export Metafile tool)

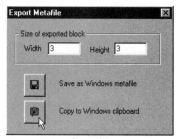

Step 15

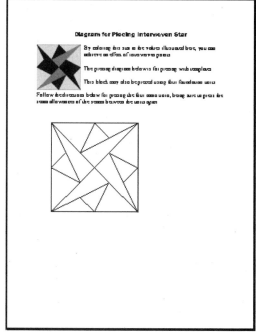

Step 16

Get **ready for the metafile**.

13 Open (or maximize) EQ4, with the Interwoven Star on the drawing board. It doesn't matter whether you have the line drawing or coloring of the block showing.

14 Click the Export Metafile button on the left toolbar.

15 For this example, 3 is fine for Width and Height. Click Copy to Windows clipboard, since we need this metafile only once.

Trick:
You may also click to Save as Windows metafile from the Export Metafile menu. I like to save my metafiles in a folder of their own in EQ4. If EQ4 does not appear in the Save in dialog box, click the down arrow and navigate to find where you saved EQ4. Click the Create New Folder button and type EQ4 Metafiles. Double-click the new folder (it will appear in the Save in dialog box). Place your cursor in the Filename dialog box, click, and type in a new name for your metafile. Click Save.

16 Open the Word document and press Ctrl+V to paste your metafile. (The block will appear as a line drawing.)

Note:
If the metafile does not paste where the cursor was when you ended typing, click FORMAT, Picture, Position tab, and click on "Float over text" to remove the check. Click OK. (This may happen in Word 97.)

Trick:
If you choose to save the drawing as a metafile, you will need to click on Insert, Picture, and find the file in one of your directories.

17 Place your cursor in the middle of the block and double-click.
Wait a few seconds and you will see a new screen with your block. You will now be using Word as a drawing program to separate units of the block and to color them.

18 The margins are tight around the block drawing, so you need to expand them to allow for the separated units you want to create. On the top ruler, position your cursor on the edge of the left margin and

EQ4 Magic   97

wait for the cursor to change to a double-ended arrow. Click, hold, and drag the double-ended arrow to the left to enlarge the margin by about 1½ inches.

🔖 Note:
If you don't see the rulers to the left and across the top of your document screen, click VIEW and Ruler.

19 Do the same to the left ruler for the top margin.

The block will tend to hug the top and left margins. Leftover space can be adjusted later.

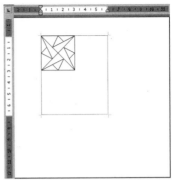
Steps 18-19

Coloring the block in gray scale

For copying purposes, grayscale will be best to designate value differences in coloring a block.

🔖 Note:
Make sure the Drawing tool bar for Word is available. To make it visible, click VIEW, point to Toolbars, and click Drawing to check that option.

20 Click the patch you want to color then click the down arrow next to the paint bucket on the Drawing toolbar. Find a value of gray and click it. The patch will be colored.

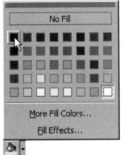

Step 20

21 Repeat step 20 to color all the parts of the star. If you want the background to remain white, you do not have to color it.

Now comes the fun of **separating the units** of the block.

22 Click away from the block to clear the cursor. Hold down the Shift key on your keyboard and click each of the patches in the lower right diagonal half of the block. You will be making 8 clicks, including 4 white patches and 4 gray. Release the Shift key. Center the cross cursor on the selected unit, click, hold, and move the unit about ¾ of an inch to the right and down. Click an open space to clear the cursor.

Step 21

23 Hold down the Shift key and click the 4 patches that will form the top-center unit (2 white ane 2 gray patches). Release the Shift key, center the cross cursor, click and move that unit ¾ of an inch to the right.

Step 22

Step 23

Step 24

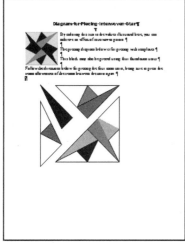

Step 25

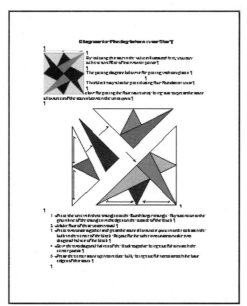

Step 26

24 Of the remaining 4 patches, click on the 3 left-edge patches (2 white and 1 gray patch) while holding down the shift key. Release the Shift key, center the cross cursor, click and move the unit ¾" down. You will have one remaining gray patch that does not need to be moved.

Tricks:

- You can edit the moves as you wish. Just remember that when you want several patches to move at the same time you must select them altogether with the Shift key.

- You may undo several past steps sequentially with Ctrl+Z.

- Move the right and bottom margins as you did in steps 18-19 if you want to tighten the space around the block.

- With the drawing tools, I added arrows to show grain line and to show which units join with others. Click the Arrow tool on the Drawing toolbar and click, hold, and drag to draw an arrow anywhere you like. With the arrow selected click the drawing tool with the three horizontal arrows (Arrow Style). Here you can select the kind of arrow points you want, whether you want a double pointed arrow (as I used for grain line), and the size of the heads and lines of the arrows. You're in control for how your printout will look.

25 FILE, Close, and return to your Word document.

Tricks:

- If you need to get back to this picture to edit more, double-click the picture.

- To center the block position your cursor in the middle of the block and click to select it. Click the alignment tool to center text and your picture will be centered between the page margins.

26 Repeat steps 10-11, including the respective Word 97 or 2000 instructions to add more text.

27 Save.

EQ4 Magic 99

Making a Lone Star Quilt

There is more than one way to design a Lone Star Quilt in EQ4. This feat of magic may be the easiest way to get not only the design of the quilt but also accurate templates. Here I will show you how to design the quilt and how to use shaded coloring for wonderful effects.

Making the Lone Star block

1   On the LIBRARIES menu, click Block Library. Double-click EQ Libraries if this book is not already open. Double-click 1 Classic Pieced, and click Eight-Point Stars.

2   Find the block called Diamond and click it. Click Copy. Click Close.

 Trick:
If you click the 4-block display button, Diamond will be the upper right block. Rest your cursor on the block without clicking and the name of the block will appear.

3   Click View Sketchbook, click the Blocks tab, and click the Diamond block.

4   Click Edit.
We will use this block as a template for drawing the Lone Star, but we will be working with only one quarter of this block. We need to delete several lines in order to do this.

5   Click the Select tool.

6   Hold down the Shift button on your keyboard and click all the lines in the block except for the lines outlining the diamonds in the upper right quadrant of the block. Press the Delete key on your keyboard. The selected lines will disappear.

7   Click the Refresh Screen tool on the left toolbar. This will eliminate any ghost lines that remain on the drawing board.

Most Lone Star quilts have at least a 6-grid of diamonds in each point. We are going to draw that grid.

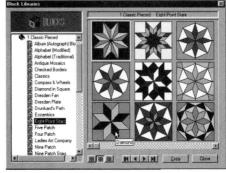

Steps 1-2

Diamond block

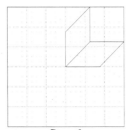

Step 6

(Edit tool)

Step 8

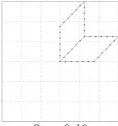

Steps 9-10

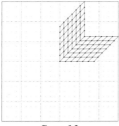

Step 13

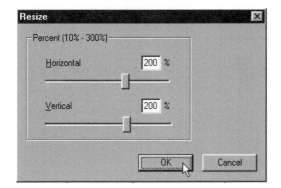

Step 17

8 Click the little black square in the lower-left corner of the Edit tool button. The Edit pop-up menu includes a dialog box to Partition. Set the number in that box to 6 by clicking the up/down arrows.

9 Click a line forming one of the diamonds to select it and click the Partition button. The line will be evenly divided into six segments.

10 Repeat this partition-ing for all the lines in the two diamonds.

11 Click the Snap to Node tool and disable all other snap-to tools. See: USING ADVANCED DRAWING FEATURES and CUSTOMIZING THE DRAWING TOOLBAR.

12 Click the Zoom In tool on the left tool bar. Drag a box (marquee) around the diamonds on the drawing board to enlarge the field for better viewing.

13 Click the Line tool. Draw lines connecting the nodes on the diamonds to form the grid of diamonds for the block. Be sure to keep your lines parallel to the edges of each diamond. Note illustration. Save in Sketchbook. Save the project.

14 Click the Fit to Window tool on the left toolbar to get your full drawing board back on the screen.

15 Press Ctrl+A to select the entire drawing on your drawing board.

16 Right-click within the worktable area to get a pop-up menu. Click Resize.

17 Type 200% for Horizontal and Vertical. Click OK.

Trick:
You can do this quickly by typing 200 in the Horizontal box, pressing the Tab key twice, and typing 200 for Vertical. Click OK.

18 On the drawing board you will see your quarter block enlarged. Click the Snap to Grid tool to enable it and disable all other snap-to tools. See: USING ADVANCED DRAWING

EQ4 Magic 101

TOOLS and CUSTOMIZING THE DRAWING TOOLBAR.

19 Click, hold, and drag the drawing carefully to fit within the block outline, with the corners of the diamonds parked in the lower left corner of the block. Note illustration. Save in Sketchbook. Save the project.

20 Click View Sketchbook, click the Blocks tab, select your newly drawn block, and click Notecard. Name the block "Quarter Lone Star." Click the X to close the Notecard. Click the block you just made a notecard for to see its name at the bottom of the Sketchbook. Click the X to close the Sketchbook. Save the project.

Coloring a Lone Star block

It is easier to work with a colored block than with a line drawing in the quilt layout. There are several ways to color this quilt for dramatic effects. One is to use an 11-step gradation from one color to another with the darkest color in the center and the lightest on the tips of the star. Or you may use a 6-step gradation from dark to light starting with dark in the center and grading the color values to light in the middle band of the diamond and then grading back to dark at the tips. Or you may want to work concentric bands of color around the star.

1 Click the Color tab at the bottom of the drawing board and color the block. Save in Sketchbook.

☆ Tips and Tricks:

• It is recommended by many quilt designers that you have a darker or medium color value in the center of the star. A light value placed in that area may give the illusion of a hole (or nothing).

• You will find it very helpful to sort the color palette you will use to color your Lone Star. See page 111 in the EQ4 Design Cookbook for directions.

• You will be very pleased to see the Extended Color Palette now available for EQ4. You will load it from the CD ROM provided with this book. It has gradations of colors, shades and tones, and tints that are perfect for coloring

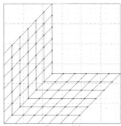

Step 19

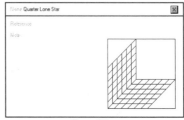

Step 20

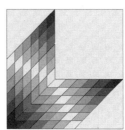

Step 1

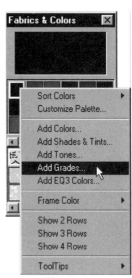

The menu you will see when you right-click a color in the Fabrics & Colors palette.

the Lone Star and other projects. See: EXPANDING THE COLOR PALETTE. Copy palette selections and sort them to appear in the front of your color palette display, as suggested above.

Laying out the Lone Star quilt in a Horizontal Quilt Layout

1   On the WORKTABLE menu, click Work on Quilt.

2   On the QUILT menu, point to New Quilt, click Horizontal.

3   Click the Layout tab.

4   In Number of blocks, click the arrows to set Horizontal 2 and Vertical 2.

5   In Size of blocks, drag the slider bars to the right end to get 48 for Width and Height. This will give your quilt a 96" center. You may choose a different measurement.

🔖 **Note:**

The 48 Width and Height may be the maximum size block set for your program. To change this, go into the FILE menu, click Preferences, and the Limits tab. There you can change the maximum size of your block by typing in another number.

✏️**Tip:**

The 48" width and height will give you a reasonable dimension for a queen size quilt. You may change this measurement according to your needs.

6   You do not want sashing so slide the slider to the far left to set a 0.00 for Width and Height.

Setting the blocks on the quilt

7   Click the Layer 1 tab.

8   Click the Set tool.

9   Click the Quarter Lone Star block and click the arrows under the block display to get the colored block.

10 Position your cursor on any block on the quilt layout. Ctrl+click will set all the blocks at once.

Steps 3-6

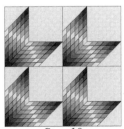

Step 10

EQ4 Magic   103

Making a Lone Star Quilt

11 Click the Rotate tool to rotate the blocks to form the Lone Star. You will rotate the lower right block one time, the lower left block two times, and the upper left block three times.

12 Save in Sketchbook. Save the project.

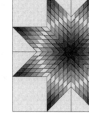

(Rotate tool)

Step 11

You can now add any border treatment you desire. See pages 28-30 of the EQ4 Design Cookbook for examples of different styles. Often a wide border of the background fabric may be desirable to make the Lone Star appear to float in the center of your quilt.

You may want to eliminate the look of the seam line in the setting triangles.

1 To do this, go to WORKTABLE and click Work on Block.

2 On the BLOCK menu, point to New Block, EasyDraw.

3 Click the Line tool. Draw a diagonal line across the block from the top left corner to the bottom right corner to form two half-square triangles.

Step 3

 Trick:
This block may be used to print out a template for the setting triangles for the Lone Star.

4 Click the Color tab and color both halves of this block the same as the background for the star. (This coloring is just for designing purposes. You will be setting this block in Layer 2 over the seam line created by your four star blocks in the quilt.) Save in Sketchbook. Save the project.

Step 4

5 On the WORLTABLE, click Work on Quilt and your Lone Star quilt will be displayed.

6 Click Layer 2 and the Set tool. Click the half-square triangle block and click the arrows under the block display to get the colored block.

7 Click, hold, and drag your cursor over the lower-right square of the quilt block in Layer 1 (you will see a dotted rectangle forming). Release the cursor and the block will pop into this space.

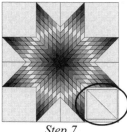

Step 7

104

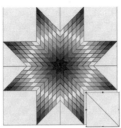

Step 9

Step 10

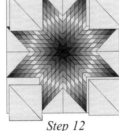

Step 12

Step 11
(Same Size tool)

Step 12

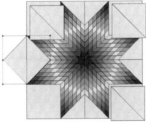

Step 14

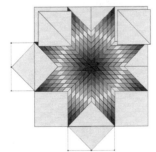

Step 15
(The lower-right setting triangle was rotated 45° and then rotated once using the Rotate tool to cover the bottom-center seam)

8 Click the Adjust tool and click the block you set.

📌 Note:
If you do not have the Graph Pad on your quilt layout screen, click VIEW and click Graph Pad. You want to have a check next to Graph Pad on the menu.

9 On the Graph Pad, make these size adjustments by clicking the arrow buttons:

- Width and Height: 28.00

Save in Sketchbook. Save project.

10 Click the Set tool and drag 3 more copies of this block.

11 To size them correctly, click the Adjust tool. Click the first block that has already been sized. Hold down the Shift key and click the other three blocks. Release Shift.

12 Click the Same Size tool on the Graph Pad to get all blocks sized correctly. Click outside the worktable to clear the cursor.

13 With the Adjust tool enabled, click one block and rotate 45 degrees with the rotation dialog box on the Graph Pad.

🎩 Trick:
Click one of the rotate arrows on the Graph Pad, the number will be highlighted, type 45.

14 Fit the block into the setting triangle, which is a half-square triangle.

15 You may need to rotate the orientation of the patches in the block, so click the Rotate tool on the right tool bar. Click the block to rotate the patches. The seam lines will no longer be obvious.

🐭 Tip:
There is a difference between rotating the *block* with the Rotation tool on the Graph Pad and rotating the *patches* with the Rotate tool on the right toolbar. When you rotate the *block* with the Rotation tool on the Graph Pad, the corners of the *block* will move along with all the patches inside the block. When you rotate the *patches* with the Rotate tool on the right toolbar, the corners of the block will remain stationary and the orientation of the patches within the block will change.

EQ4 Magic 105

16 Repeat this procedure to cover up the seams in all four setting triangles. Save in Sketchbook. Save project.

17 Click the Adjust tool and click one of the four setting triangle blocks. If you want to "trim up" the edges of your quilt, click the appropriate clip button.

⋇ Trick:
On the far right side of the Graph Pad are three buttons. The one on the left is the default button and it leaves the block overhanging the edge of the quilt. The middle one is Clip to Border and will cut the block off at the outside edge of the quilt when clicked. The right button is Clip to Center Rectangle and will cut the block off inside the first border around the center when clicked.

18 Click the next setting triangle block. Click the left clip tool to refresh the tool then click your clip tool of choice.

↳ Note:
You need to refresh the Clip-to tool after each use.

19 Do the same for the other two setting triangles blocks.

20 Save in Sketchbook. Save the project.

Coloring a Lone Star Quilt

Even though you have already colored this quilt by coloring the block, there are several ways to color this quilt for dramatic effects. Since you now see the entire finished quilt, you may want to recolor it for different visual effects.

- You can use an 11-step gradation from one color to another with the darkest color in the center and the lightest on the tips of the star.

- Or you may use a 6-step gradation from dark to light starting with dark in the center and grading the color values to light in the middle band of the diamond and then grading back to dark at the tips.

- Or you may want to work concentric bands of color around the star.

- Random scrapbag print selections can make for a busy yet interesting effect.

- You can save time coloring the Lone Star quilt. Press the Ctrl key as you color each patch. You will automatically color all four blocks in the quilt simultaneously.

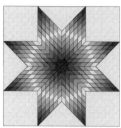
Step 16

Step 17

Other color variations of finished Lone Star Quilts

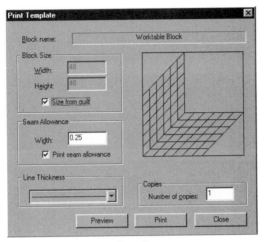

Step 2

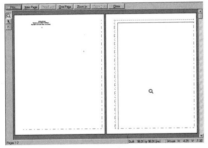

Step 3

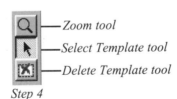

— *Zoom tool*

— *Select Template tool*

— *Delete Template tool*

Step 4

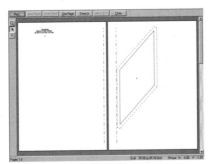

Step 7

Printing out the templates for this quilt - A Disappearing Trick

✏️**Tip:**

Because the size of the block in this quilt is so large, printing out the templates may take several sheets of paper.

🎩**Trick:**

When you load the CD ROM that comes with this book, you will enhance your EQ4 program and you will now be able to *delete templates you do not want to print.*

1   On the quilt worktable, click the Select tool and click the Quarter Lone Star block.

2   On the FILE menu, point to Print, click Templates. Set the size of the block as "Size from quilt" (a check should be in the box). Click Print seam allowance to check that option (.25 inches is the default width).

3   Click Preview.
As you view the preview pages (what you see will differ due to printers and their setups, but I have 27 pages) you will see many blank pages and some that include a few outlines. These pages are the outline of the block. You don't need the outline, only the diamonds.

4   On the top of the left toolbar you will see three icons: the top is the Zoom tool, the middle is the Select Template tool, and the bottom one is the Delete Template tool. Click the Select Template tool.

5   Click the template(s) you do not wish to print. (I clicked what looks like the beginning of a square outline on page 2.)

6   Click the Delete Template tool, and your template will disappear.

7   Repeat steps 5-6 until you see the diamonds and click Print.
I ended up with only two pages instead of 27 - presto, I think I saved a tree from disappearing.

EQ4 Magic   107

Printing out the templates for the setting half-square triangles

1 On the quilt worktable, click the Select tool, click Layer 2, and click a half-square triangle block you used to cover up the seam lines.

2 On the FILE menu, point to Print, click Templates. Set the size of the block as "Size from quilt." Click Print seam allowance to check that option.

3 Click Preview. If all looks well, click Print.

 Tips and Tricks:

- Since this printout will take a fair amount of paper, though not a lot of ink, I often use recycled copy paper for this kind of a print job. It already has printing on one side, but that's not objectionable here. Then I sort of feel like the paper is free.

- Construction tip: The longest side of the setting triangles should be cut on the straight-of-grain of your fabric in order to avoid having stretchy bias edges on the quilt.

- Cutting tip: Cut the side setting triangles as an X on a square in order to get four triangles with the straight grain along the longest side. This square should measure 1 1/4" larger than the finished measurement for the corner setting squares. With your X cut you will then have the properly sized triangles, including seam allowances.

Making a Lone Star Quilt with One Block

To draw the Lone Star as one block rather than as the quarter block, try this:

- After step 15 of the drawing instructions, click the square in the corner of the Select tool to get the Symmetry menu.

- Click Clone and Rot 90. Drag and park the unit in the lower right of the block. It's okay to overlap common lines between these two units as you park the new unit.

- Press Ctrl+A to select all. Click Clone and Flip H. Park this unit on the left side of the block. Again, it's okay to overlap common lines.

  Save in Sketchbook. Save the project.

- A disadvantage for using one block for the entire quilt is that you will have to color each patch individually, but there are no seam lines.

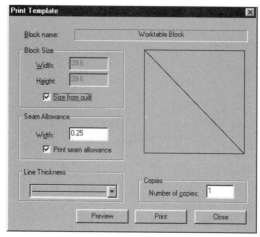

Step 2

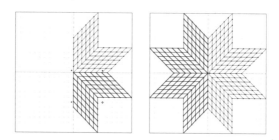

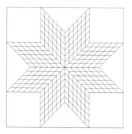

Introducing Templates

Making new quilt layout styles

EQ4 comes with quilt layouts. But you can also make your own. By setting plain blocks into layer 2, you can create a custom quilt layout to pop blocks into.

Want a large central diamond, surrounded by smaller blocks? You can do it. Want four central squares, surrounded by on-point blocks? No problem! The next six lessons all introduce new quilt layouts.

Making custom layouts isn't quick. But here's the magic. Once you make a layout, you can use and re-use the layout for quilt after quilt, getting surprisingly different designs depending on the blocks you choose.

To save a layout you can reuse:

1 Save the layout as a project.

2 When you want to use this layout to make a new quilt, open the project, use Save as to give the project a new name, then save your new quilt in this new project.

EQ4 Magic   109

Making a Diamond Quilt Layout

1 On the WORKTABLE menu, click Work on Block.

2 On the BLOCK menu, point to New Block, click EasyDraw.

3 Click the Color tab. Color the square using a dark color such as red.

4 Save in Sketchbook. Answer Yes in the question box. Save the project.

5 On the LIBRARIES menu, click Block Library. Double-click EQ Libraries if this book is not already open. Double-click 1 Classic Pieced, and click Diamond in Square.

6 Find the block called Diamond in the Square and click it. Click Copy. Click Close.

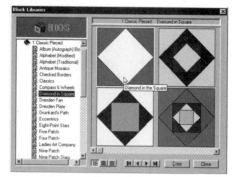

Steps 5-6

Trick:
If you click the 4-block display button, Diamond in the Square will be the top-left block. Rest your cursor on the block without clicking and the name of the block will appear.

7 Click View Sketchbook, click the Blocks tab, and click the Diamond in the Square block.

8 Click Edit.

9 Click the dark square in the corner of the Edit tool to get the Edit menu.

10 Click one of the lines in the diamond and click Half. Repeat for the other three lines of the diamond.

11 Click the Snap to Node tool. No other snap-to tools should be enabled. See: USING ADVANCED DRAWING FEATURES and CUSTOMIZING THE DRAWING TOOLBARS.

12 Click the Line tool.

13 Draw two lines connecting the opposite nodes that were created in step 6. (Note illustration.)

Step 6
(Diamond in the Square)

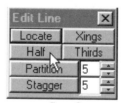

Step 9

Step 13

Step 17

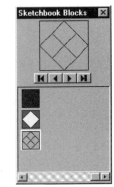

Step 19

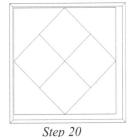

(Set tool)

Step 20

Step 21
(Adjust tool)

Step 22

Step 22

14 Save in Sketchbook. Save the project.

15 On the WORKTABLE menu, click Work on Quilt.

16 On the QUILT menu, point to New Quilt, click Country Set.

17 Click the Layout tab. Slide the bar to set 24 for Width and 24 for Height. *Or* you may highlight the number for Width and type in 24. Press the Tab key twice on your keyboard and type 24 for Height.

18 Click the Layer 3 tab.

19 Click the Set tool. Click the Diamond in the Square block that has the X in the middle from the Sketchbook Blocks display.

20 Click, hold, and drag the cursor from the top-left corner of the quilt layout (not including the borders) down to the bottom-right corner to set the block. Release the mouse and the block will pop into the space. (A block set in Layer 3 will always appear as an outline with no color.)

✎ Note:
If you do not have the Graph Pad on your quilt layout screen, click VIEW and click Graph Pad. You want to have a check mark next to Graph Pad on the menu.

21 Click the Adjust tool. Click the block you set in the quilt.

22 On the Graph Pad, make the following adjustments:

- Horizontal location (top box on far left of Graph Pad): 0.00

- Vertical location (bottom box on far left of Graph Pad): 0.00

- Size width (top box in center of Graph Pad): 24.00

- Size height (bottom box in center of Graph Pad): 24.00

23 Save in Sketchbook. Save the project.

EQ4 Magic 111

Making a Diamond Quilt Layout

Tip:
This block was placed in Layer 3 because it
will be an outline pattern for placing blank
blocks in Layer 2. Layer 3 is usually the layer
reserved for quilt patterns to position over a
quilt top. Here we're using it for a guide. When
we're ready to get rid of it as a guide, we can
simply go into Layer 3, select the block with
the Adjust tool, and press the Delete key on
the keyboard.

24 Click the Layer 2 tab. Click the Select tool.

Trick:
The reason we're using Layer 2 to set the
blocks is so that we can place a block in Layer
1 for a background later.

25 Click the blank block in the Sketchbook
Blocks display. Click the right-arrow button
to get the dark colored version.

26 Click, hold, and drag 4 dark blocks anywhere on the quilt layout.

27 Click the Adjust tool. Click one of the
blocks you just set.

28 On the Graph Pad, make the following size
adjustments:

• Size width: 8.50

• Size height: 8.50

29 With the block still selected, hold down the
Shift key on your keyboard as you click the
other three blocks. Release the Shift key.
Click the Same Size button on the Graph
Pad.

30 Click in a free space on the worktable away
from the blocks to clear the cursor.

31 Click one of the newly-sized blocks. Click
an arrow next to the Rotate box on the
Graph Pad. Type 45.

32 Repeat step 31 for the other three blocks so
they are all on-point.

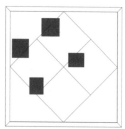

Step 26

Step 28

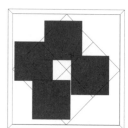

Step 29

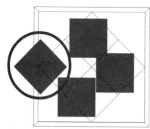

Step 31

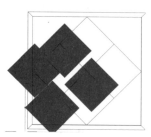

Step 32

112

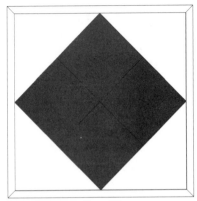

Step 33

33 Click the on-point blocks one at a time and using the Graph Pad position one block for each of the following locations.

A) The top block should have these position locations:

- Horizontal location: 12.00
- Vertical location: 0.00

B) The right block should have these position locations:

- Horizontal location: 18.00
- Vertical location: 6.00

C) The bottom block should have these position locations:

- Horizontal location: 12.00
- Vertical location: 12.00

D) The left block should have these position locations:

- Horizontal location: 6.00
- Vertical location: 6.00

34 Save in Sketchbook. Save the project.

 **Tips and Tricks:**

- **Gather blocks to set into the Layer 2 diamonds. Select a block, place the cursor in the center of any of the Layer 2 blocks, and click to set.**

- **With this template, you can add or change border styles and sizes without disturbing the center layout. But you cannot change the size of the center rectangle of the quilt without disturbing the center layout.**

- **For the illustration quilts, blocks were set in Layer 1 so they would be background to the blocks set in the diamond.**

Examples of quilts using the Diamond layout.

EQ4 Magic   **113**

Making a Diamond Quilt Layout

Making a Tilted-Block Quilt Layout

Here is a quilt layout that you can save as a template/file for many designing possibilities. It uses a square block set at an angle that is not "on-point" (45° rotation), so I call it "Tilt." You will use Layer 1 and Layer 2 in a Horizontal quilt layout for this tilt-block quilt layout. Blocks that will be set in Layer 1 may be chosen from the Twists page of Paper Piecing blocks in the EQ4 Block Library. There are 25 blocks in that category, each offering a different layout possibility for Tilt.

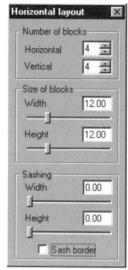

Steps 3-9

1   On the WORKTABLE menu, click Work on Quilt.

2   On the QUILT menu, point to New Quilt, click Horizontal.

3   Click the Layout tab. Under Number of Blocks, click the up or down arrows to get 4 for Horizontal. Press the Tab key on your keyboard.

4   Type 4 for Vertical. Press Tab.

5   For Size of blocks, type 12.00 for Width. Press Tab twice.

6   Type 12.00 for Height. Press Tab twice.

7   Type 0.00 for Sashing Width. Press Tab twice.

8   Type 0.00 for Sashing Height.

9   Click to remove the check next to Sash border (if there is one there).

10 Click the Layer 1 tab.

11 On the LIBRARIES menu, click Block Library. Double-click EQ Libraries if this book is not already open. Double-click 3 Paper Piecing, and click Twists.

12 Find the block called Twist V and click it. Click Copy.

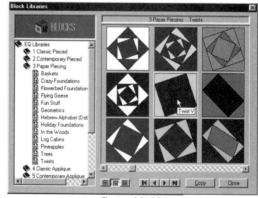

Steps 11-12

*Step 12
(Twist V)*

✨ **Trick:**
If you click the 9-block display button, Twist V will be in the middle of the display. Rest your cursor on the block without clicking and

Step 15
(Stars and Stripes)

Step 16
(Flying Stars)

Step 18

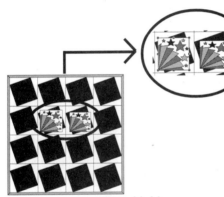

Steps 20-21

Step 22
(Adjust tool)

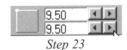

Step 23

Step 25
(Same size tool)

the name of name of the block will appear.

13 Go back to the Block Library menu on the left side of the screen and scroll down to the book named 8 Overlaid Blocks. Double-click this book.

14 Click Simple Designs.

15 Click the Stars and Stripes block. Click Copy.

16 Click the Flying Stars block. Click Copy. Click Close.

17 Click the Set tool. Click the Twist V block in the Sketchbook Blocks display.

18 Position your cursor in the center of any block space on the quilt layout. Ctrl+click to fill the quilt.

19 Click the Layer 2 tab.

20 Click the Flying Stars block. Anywhere on the quilt worktable click, hold, and drag the cursor to draw a box (marquee). Release the mouse and the block will pop into the space.

21 Repeat step 20 for a second block.

22 Click the Adjust tool. Click one of the Flying Stars blocks on your quilt.

Note:
If you do not have the Graph Pad on your quilt layout screen, click VIEW and click Graph Pad. You want to have a check mark next to Graph Pad on the menu.

23 Note the sizing of the block in the boxes in the middle of the Graph Pad. Click the arrows to make the block size 9.50 width and height (top and bottom boxes respectively).

24 With the block you just sized still selected, hold down the Shift key on your keyboard and click on the unsized Flying Stars block. Release the Shift key.

25 Click the Same Size tool on the graph pad to make both blocks the same size.

EQ4 Magic 115

Making a Tilted-Block Quilt Layout

26 Click in a free space on teh worktable away from the blocks to clear your cursor.

27 Click once again on one of the blocks to select it. Drag it until the top-left corner of the block matches the top-left corner of the square in the center of the Twist V block.

28 You will use the Rotate tool on the Graph Pad. Click the left arrow to get -19°.

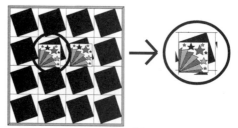

Step 27

🍴 Note:

You will be rotating counterclockwise, so you need to get a *negative number* in this box. Because you cannot type a negative number here, you must use the arrow button.

Step 28

💥 Tricks:

- Notice how your block is starting to tilt. 19 degrees counterclockwise should get it into the right position to park it over the square of the Twist V block. Yet, you may want to finely tune or set the block. Click the Adjust tool and click the block you just rotated. Click, hold, and drag a corner of the block to stretch it to fill in the center space of the Twist V block.

- It is helpful to use the Zoom In tool for lining up the Flying Stars block to the Twist V block. Click the Fit to Window tool to return to the whole quilt.

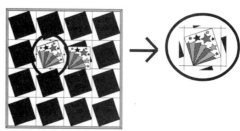

Step 28

29 Click the Set tool (the Flying Stars block should be selected). Click, hold, and drag to set another block on the quilt worktable. Repeat 13 more times.

30 Click the Adjust tool. Click the second block you sized in steps 21-25 (the block that has not been rotated).

31 With the correctly sized block selected first, hold down the Shift key on your keyboard and click all of the new blocks from step 28.

32 Click the Same Size tool on the Graph Pad to resize all of the blocks at one time.

33 Repeat steps 26-27 for the remaining blocks.

34 Save in Sketchbook. Save the project.

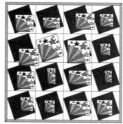 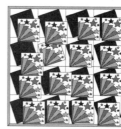

Step 29   *Steps 30-32*

Step 33

Making a Tilted-Block Quilt Layout

Using the Stars and Stripes block

35 Click View Sketchbook. Click the Quilts tab and click Notecard if your new quilt design is on display. Write any notes about your quilt on this Notecard. Close the X to close the Notecard. Click the X to close the Sketchbook. Save the project again.

You may color on the quilt and highlight interesting secondary designs. Change the borders, if you like. Add more borders.

When you're ready, go back into Layer 2 of the quilt and click the Set tool. Click the Stars and Stripes block. Position your cursor *in the center of any block* in Layer 2 and Ctrl+click. The Stars and Strips block will be set into every block area where you previously had the Flying Stars blocks. The quilt layout you designed will act as a template for future use because you can so easily replace the blocks you worked to position in this quilt.

Remember that there are 24 more blocks in the Twists category in the Block Library, that you can use with this technique.

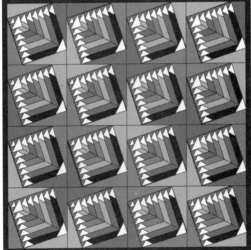

Using the Rainbow Logs block
(2 Contemporary Pieced, Log Cabin-Like)

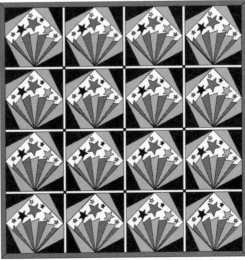

Using Twist XVI block in Layer 1

EQ4 Magic 117

Using a Block as a Quilt Layout Template

Here's one example of a quilt template: a new quilt layout style to use and reuse. To make this new layout style, you can use a block - enlarging the block until it's quilt-sized, then setting blocks into the block patches - using Layer 2. Draw these simple blocks for an example.

Block 1

1   On the WORKTABLE menu, click Work on Block.

2   On the BLOCK menu, point to New Block, click on EasyDraw.

3   Click the Color tab and color this blank block white. Save in Sketchbook, and answer Yes to the question.

Block 2

4   Click the EasyDraw tab.

5   On the BLOCK menu, click Drawing Board Setup.

6   For the Snap to Grid Points, use the up/ down arrows to get 27 Horizontal. Press the Tab key on your keyboard.

7   For Vertical, type in 27. Press Tab.

8   For Block Size Horizontal, type in 9. Press Tab.

9   For Vertical, type in 9. Click OK.

⤷ Note:
If you don't see the rulers to the left and across the top of your document screen, click VIEW and Ruler.

10   Click the Line tool. Draw a vertical line starting from the 5" ruler marking on top down to the 5" ruler marking on the left. (The line will not touch the left side of the block, but the end will be even with the left 5" marking. Note the illustration.)

11   Draw a horizontal line at the 1" marking on the left ruler starting from the vertical line and ending at the right side of the block.

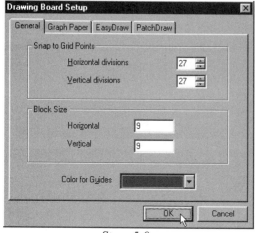

Steps 5-9

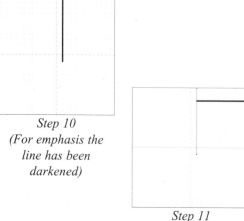

Step 10
(For emphasis the line has been darkened)

Step 11

118

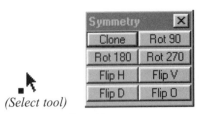

(Select tool)

Step 13

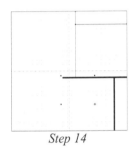

Step 14

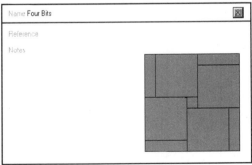

Step 17

12 Press Ctrl+A to select both lines.

13 Click the dark square in the bottom-left corner of the Select tool to get the Symmetry pop-up menu. Click Clone and then Rot 90.

14 Click, hold, and drag the new figure and park it so the longer line (which is now horizontal) is lined up with the 5" mark on the left ruler and the right end touches the right side of the block. Note illustration.

15 Press Ctrl+A to select all lines.

16 On the Symmetry menu (click the dark square in the corner of the Select tool button if it is no longer displayed), click Clone and then Rot 180.

17 Click, hold, and drag the figure and park it on the left side of the block. The ends of all lines should touch either the side of the block or the lines of the first half of the block.

18 Save in Sketchbook. Save the project.

19 Click the Color tab and color all the patches of this block in any one dark solid color (red works well).

20 Save in Sketchbook.

21 Click View Sketchbook. Click the Blocks tab. Click the block you just drew. Click Notecard.

Trick:
To see the colored version of this block, click the arrow keys at the bottom of the Sketchbook display.

22 Name this block "Four Bits" or anything else that strikes your fancy. Type in any other notes you may want to record. Click X to close the Notecard. (Click the block you just made a notecard for to see its name at the bottom of the Sketchbook.) Click the X to close the Sketchbook.

23 Save the project.

Step 22

EQ4 Magic **119**

Using a Block as a Quilt Layout Template

24 Save the block in My Library.

🖈 **Note:**

To save a block in My Library, follow the directions on pages 56-57 of the EQ4 Design Cookbook. I would recommend naming a library Style as "Quilt Layout Templates" and keeping a collection of block possibilities stored there.

Setting up the Quilt

1 On the WORKTABLE menu, click Work on Quilt.

2 On the QUILT menu, point to New Quilt, click Country Set.

3 Click the Layout tab. Slide the bar to set 45 for Width and 45 for Height. *Or* you may highlight the number for Width and type in 45. Press the Tab key twice on your keyboard and type 45 for Height.

4 Click the Layer 1 tab.

5 Click the Set tool. Click the Four Bits block in the Sketchbook Blocks display. Find the colored version by clicking the right-arrow button.

6 Click, hold, and drag the cursor from the top-left corner of the quilt layout (do not include the borders) down to the bottom-right corner to set the block. Release the mouse and the block will pop into the space.

🖈 **Note:**

If you do not have the Graph Pad on your quilt layout screen, click VIEW and click Graph Pad. You want to have a check mark next to Graph Pad on the menu.

7 Click the Adjust tool. Click the block you set in the quilt.

8 On the Graph Pad, make the following adjustments:

- Horizontal location (top box on far left of Graph Pad): 0.00

- Vertical location (bottom box on far left of Graph Pad): 0.00

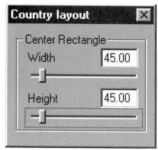

Step 3

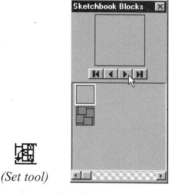

(Set tool)

Step 5

Step 6

Step 8

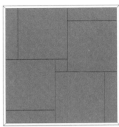

Step 8

Step 12

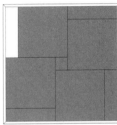

Step 14

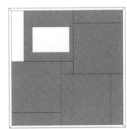

Step 16

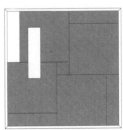

Step 19

- Size width (top box in center of Graph Pad): 45.00

- Size height (bottom box in center of Graph Pad): 45.00

9 Save in Sketchbook. Save the project.

10 Click the Layer 2 tab.

11 Click the Set tool. Click the blank block in the Sketchbook Blocks display. Click the right-arrow button to get the white colored version.

12 Take a look at the vertical rectangle in the upper-left corner of the quilt. Click, hold, and drag a box to cover that rectangle. (See why you colored the blank block in contrast to the template block?)

13 Click the Adjust tool (to make some size and position adjustments). Click the white block you just set.

14 On the Graph Pad, make the following adjustments:

- Horizontal location: 0.00

- Vertical location: 0.00

- Size Width: 5.00

- Size Height: 20.00

15 Click the Set tool again. Click the white block in the Sketchbook block display.

16 Click, hold, and drag a box any size onto the dark of the quilt.

17 Click the Adjust tool. Click the first block you adjusted for size.

18 Hold down the Shift key on your keyboard and click the second block you just set. Both blocks will be highlighted with nodes. Release the Shift key.

19 On the Graph Pad, click the Same Size button. (If you rest your cursor on the box without clicking, you will see a message label on the bottom bar on your worktable.) The two blocks will now be the same size.

EQ4 Magic 121

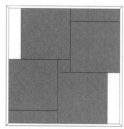

Step 21

🔖 **Note:**

It is important to click the block that has already been adjusted first. Then click the block that is to be sized the same.

20 Click in a free space on the worktable away from the blocks to clear the cursor.

21 Click the block you just sized and using the Graph Pad, make the following position-location adjustments:

- Horizontal: 40.00

- Vertical: 25.00

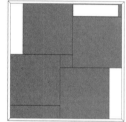

Step 23

22 Click the Set tool. The white block in the Sketchbook Blocks display should be selected.

23 Click, hold, and drag a box to cover the horizontal rectangle at the top right of the base template.

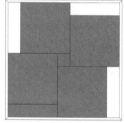

Step 25

24 Click the Adjust tool. Click the block you just set.

25 On the Graph Pad, make the following adjustments:

- Horizontal location: 25.00

- Vertical location: 0.00

- Width: 20.00

- Height: 5.00

26 Click the Set tool.

27 Drag a box to set a block any size.

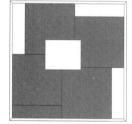

Step 27

28 Click the Adjust tool. Click the horizontal rectangle block you sized in step 25. Hold down the Shift key on your keyboard and click the block you set in step 27. Release the Shift key.

29 Click the Same Size button on the far right of the Graph Pad. Click an open space away from the blocks to clear the cursor.

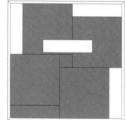

Step 29

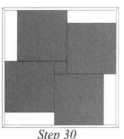

Step 30

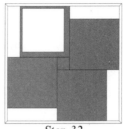

Step 32

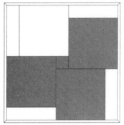

Step 34

Step 36

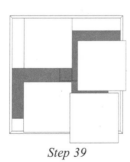

Step 39

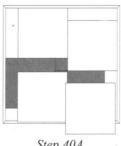

Step 40A

30 Click the block you just sized. Using the Graph Pad, make the following position-location adjustments:

- Horizontal location: 0.00
- Vertical location: 40.00

31 Click the Set tool.

32 Drag a box to set a square block into a square space in the upper left part of the layout template in Layer 1.

33 Click the Adjust tool. Click the square you set in the previous step.

34 On the Graph Pad, make the following adjustments:

- Horizontal location: 5.00
- Vertical location: 0.00
- Width: 20.00
- Height: 20.00

35 Click the Set tool.

36 Drag three more squares, any size (these blocks will be covering the remaining large squares on Layer 1).

37 Click the Adjust tool. Click the block you sized in step 34.

38 Hold down the Shift key as you click all three of the blocks you set in step 36. Release the Shift key.

39 Click the Same Size tool. Clear the cursor.

40 Click the newly-sized blocks one at a time and position one block for each of the following locations.

A) The upper-right block should have these position locations:

- Horizontal location: 25.00
- Vertical location: 5.00

EQ4 Magic 123

B) The lower-right block should have these position locations:

- Horizontal: 20.00
- Vertical: 25.00

C) The lower-left block should have these position locations:

- Horizontal: 0.00
- Vertical: 20.00

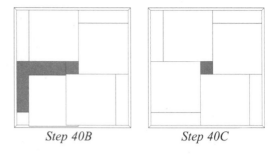

Step 40B   *Step 40C*

41 Click the Set tool. Drag one last block to cover the center square on Layer 1.

42 Click the Adjust tool. Click the block you just set.

43 On the Graph Pad, make these adjustments:

- Horizontal: 20.00
- Vertical: 20.00
- Height: 5.00
- Width: 5.00

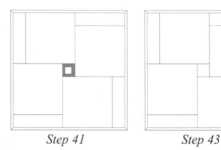

Step 41   *Step 43*

44 Save in Sketchbook.

45 Click View Sketchbook. Click the Quilts tab.

46 Click the far-right arrow to get the most recently saved quilt. Click Notecard.

47 Type in the name, "Four Bits Quilt Template" and any other notes you may want to add.

48 Click the X to close the Notecard.

49 Click the X to close the Sketchbook.

50 Save the project.

Step 45-46

Tips and Tricks:

- Gather blocks to set into the Layer 2 rectangles. Select a block, place the cursor *in the center* of any of the Layer 2 blocks, and click to set.

- Size the quilt according to the size of the square blocks you want to use. The overall dimension is 2 times the size of the block plus ¼ of the size of the block. For example, if you want to use a 12" block, you would take 2 x 12 = 24, plus ¼ of 12, which is 3, and get an overall size of 27".

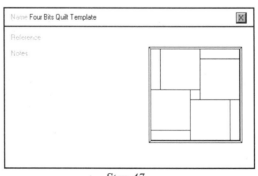

Step 47

Examples of quilts using the block quilt layout template.

- With this template, you can add or change border styles and sizes without disturbing the center layout. But you cannot change the size of the center rectangle of the quilt without disturbing the center layout.

- Check the EQ4 Classic Pieced Library for more blocks that would be appropriate for a quilt layout template. See "Flying Squares" and "Children's Delight" in the Five Patch category; "Carrie Nation Quilt" in the Four Patch category; and "Domino" in the Ladies Art Company category. Look for blocks that have mostly four-sided patches (squares, rectangles, diamonds).

- For the illustration quilt (below), I used a 6"-wide border, Corner style and the following blocks from the EQ4 Libraries:
  - "Diamond in the Square" from 1 Classic Pieced, Simple Blocks
  - "Flying Geese V" from 3 Paper Piecing, Flying Geese Library
  - "Roses and Butterfly" from 5 Contemporary Applique, Flowers

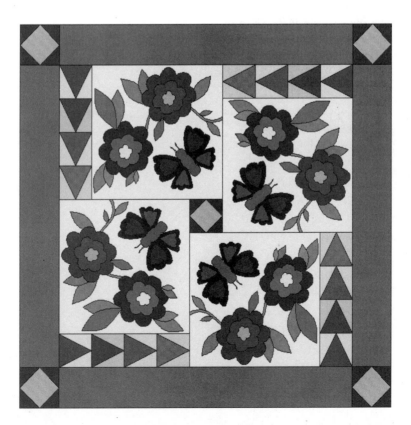

EQ4 Magic 125

Making a Temple Court Quilt Layout

The "Temple Court" block is an example of a good block to use for a quilt layout template. It is especially interesting for quilt design because it has areas that are horizontal as well as on-point for block placement. There are some tricks to setting up this block as a template that I would like to show to you. Please review USING A BLOCK AS A QUILT LAYOUT TEMPLATE before doing this lesson.

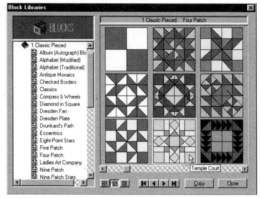

Steps 1-2

1 On the LIBRARIES menu, click Block Library. Double-click EQ Libraries if this book is not already open. Double-click 1 Classic Pieced, and click Four Patch.

2 Find the block called Temple Court and click it. Click Copy. Click Close.

✨ Trick:
If you click the 9-block display button, Temple Court will be in the middle of the bottom row. Rest your cursor on the block without clicking and the name of the block will appear.

3 Click View Sketchbook. Click the Blocks tab.

4 Click the Temple Court block. Click Edit. Take a moment to study the grid pattern for this block. Although the drawing grid was set for 24, it could have also been set for 8. We'll use multiples of 8, then, to set up the quilt size.

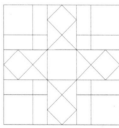

Step 4
(Temple Court block)

5 Click the Color tab. Color all the block's patches in a dark solid color, such as red. Save in Sketchbook.

6 On the BLOCK menu, point to New Block, click EasyDraw.

7 Click the Color tab. Color the blank block white. Save in Sketchbook. Answer Yes in the question box.

8 On the WORKTABLE menu, click Work on Quilt.

9 On the QUILT menu, point to New Quilt, click Country Set.

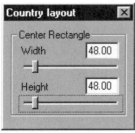

Step 9

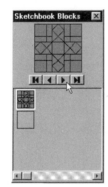

(Set tool)

Step 11

Step 12

Step 14

Step 18

9 Click the Layout tab. Slide the bar to set 48 for Width and 48 for Height. *Or* you may highlight the number for Width and type in 48. Press the Tab key twice and type in 48 for Height.

10 Click the Layer 1 tab.

11 Click the Set tool. Click the Temple Court block in the Sketchbook Blocks display. Click the right-arrow button to get the colored version.

12 Click, hold, and drag the cursor from the top-left corner of the quilt layout (do not include the borders) down to the bottom-right corner to set the block. Release the mouse and the block will pop into the space.

Note:
If you do not have the Graph Pad on your quilt layout screen, click VIEW and click Graph Pad. You want to have a check mark next to Graph Pad on the menu.

13 Click the Adjust tool. Click the block you set in the quilt.

14 On the Graph Pad, make the following adjustments:

- Horizontal location (top box on far left of Graph Pad): 0.00

- Vertical location (bottom box on far left of Graph Pad): 0.00

- Size width (top box in center of Graph Pad): 48.00

- Size height (bottom box in center of Graph Pad): 48.00

15 Save in Sketchbook. Save the project.

16 Click the Layer 2 tab.

17 Click the Set tool. Click the blank block that you colored. Click the right-arrow button to get the colored version.

18 Click, hold, and drag a box any size onto the quilt.

EQ4 Magic 127

19 Click the Adjust tool. Click the block you just set.

20 On the Graph Pad, make the following adjustments:

- Horizontal location: 0.00
- Vertical location: 0.00
- Size width: 12.00
- Size height: 12.00

21 Click the Set tool. Drag three more white blocks onto the quilt.

22 Click the Adjust tool. Click the first block you sized in step 20. Hold down the Shift key as you click the other three blocks. Release the Shift key. Click the Same Size button on the far right of the Graph Pad.

23 Click in a free space on the worktable away from the blocks to clear the cursor.

24 Click, hold, and drag each block separately you sized in step 22 and set them over the squares in the corners of the base block in Layer 1. (We will not bother with finely tuned accurate placement yet.)

25 Click the Set tool. Drag four more white blocks onto the quilt (they will be the vertical rectangles).

26 Click the Adjust tool. Click one of the blocks you just set.

27 On the Graph Pad make the following size adjustments:

- Width: 6.00
- Height: 12.00

28 With this block still selected, hold down the Shift key as you click the other three blocks from step 25. Release the Shift key. Click the Same Size button on the Graph Pad. Clear the cursor.

29 Click, hold, and drag each block separately you set in step 25 into position to cover the vertical rectangles on the base block in Layer 1.

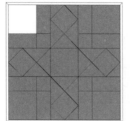
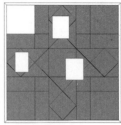

Step 20   *Step 21*

Step 22

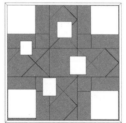

Step 25

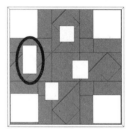

Step 27

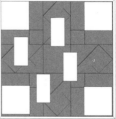

Step 28

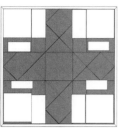

Step 31

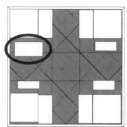

Step 33

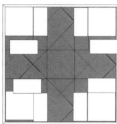

Step 34

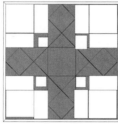

Step 37

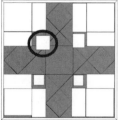

Step 39

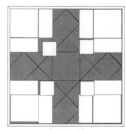

Step 40

Step 43

30 Save in Sketchbook. Save the project.

31 Click the Set tool. Drag four more white blocks onto the quilt (they will be the horizontal rectangles).

32 Click the Adjust tool. Click one of the blocks you just set.

33 On the Graph Pad make the following size adjustments:

- Width: 12.00

- Height: 6.00

34 With this block still selected, hold down the Shift key as you click the other three blocks you set in step 31. Release the Shift key. Click the Same Size button on the Graph Pad. Clear the cursor.

35 Click, hold, and drag each block separately you set in step 31 into position to cover the horizontal rectangles on the base block in Layer 1.

36 Save in Sketchbook. Save the project.

37 Click the Set tool. Drag four more white blocks onto the quilt (they will be the small squares).

38 Click the Adjust tool. Click one of the blocks you just set.

39 On the Graph Pad make the Width and Height 6.00.

40 With this block still selected, hold down the Shift key and click the other three blocks you set in step 37. Release the Shift key. Click the Same Size button on the Graph Pad. Clear the cursor.

41 Click, hold, and drag each block separately you set in step 37 to cover the small squares on the base block in Layer 1.

42 Save in Sketchbook. Save the project.

43 Click the Set tool. Drag one large block onto the quilt. (This block will be the on-point square in the center.)

EQ4 Magic 129

44 Click the Adjust tool. Click the block you just set.

45 On the Graph Pad, make the Width and Height 17.00.

46 With the large square block selected, click an arrow next to the Rotate box on the Graph Pad (to highlight the number in the box). Type 45.

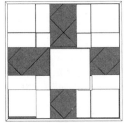
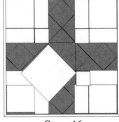

Step 45   *Step 46*

47 Click, hold, and drag the square, now on-point, to cover the center of the quilt layout.

48 Click the Set tool. Drag four more white blocks onto the quilt (they will be the smaller on-point squares).

49 Click the Adjust tool. Click one of the blocks you just set.

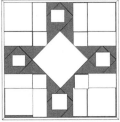

Step 48

50 On the Graph Pad, make the Width and Height 8.50.

51 With this block still selected, hold down the Shift key and click the other three blocks you set in step 48. Release the Shift key. Click the Same Size button on the Graph Pad. Clear the cursor.

52 Click one resized block (from steps 50 or 51). Click an arrow next to the Rotate box on the Graph Pad. Type 45.

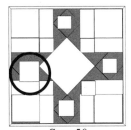
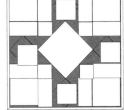

Step 50   *Step 51*

53 Repeat step 52 for the other three same-sized blocks so they are all on-point.

54 Click, hold, and drag the smaller on-point squares to cover the same small squares on the base block in Layer 1.

55 Click the Set tool. Drag one more block onto the quilt.

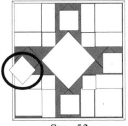
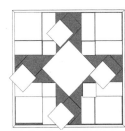

Step 52   *Step 53*

56 Click the Adjust tool. Click a square in any of the corners of the quilt layout. Hold down the Shift key and click the square from step 55. Click the Same Size button on the Graph Pad. Clear the cursor.

57 Click, hold, and drag the block to fit over the square on point in the center.

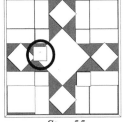

Step 55   *Step 56*

Step 60

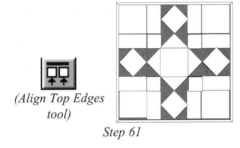

(Align Top Edges tool)

Step 61

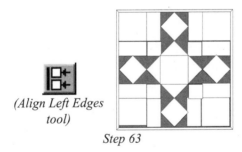

(Align Left Edges tool)

Step 63

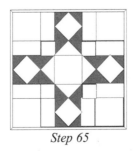

Step 65

58 Save in Sketchbook. Save the project.

Use the Align tools on the Graph Pad to position the blocks in Layer 2.
(Remember, you will only be aligning the white blocks.)

59 **Top row**: Click the Adjust tool. Click the top-left block. Hold down the Shift key as you click the other blocks across the top row, including the square on-point. Release the Shift key.

60 On the Graph Pad, click the Align tool with the horizontal line over two squares. This will bring all the selected blocks into alignment with the top of the first block selected. The Vertical locator box (the bottom box) will read 0.00 for each of these blocks. Clear the cursor.

61 To position the blocks horizontally, from left to right, use these locator readings in the top box:

• 0.00, 12.00, 24.00, 30.00, 36.00.

62 **Left column**: Click the top left block. Hold down the shift key as you click the other blocks down the left column, *not including the square on-point.* Release the Shift key.

63 On the Graph Pad, click the Align tool with the vertical line to the left of two squares. This will bring all the selected blocks into a left side alignment with the first square selected. The Horizontal locator box (the top box) will read 0.00 for each of these blocks except the square on-point. Clear the cursor.

64 Click the square on-point to make the horizontal locator 6.00.

65 To position the blocks vertically, from top to bottom, use these locator readings in the bottom box:

• 0.00, 12.00, 18.00 (for the square on point), 30.00, 36.00.

EQ4 Magic   131

66 You may use the positions of the blocks in the top row and the left column to line up the rest of the blocks. Look at the quilt and find alignment landmarks in common. Be sure to click the blocks that are already correctly placed before selecting any other blocks, because the first block selected is the reference block. Note that you can align the squares on-point with tops, bottoms, and sides of the horizontal squares. Careful placement of all these squares is important.

To position the large center on-point square, line up the left side point with the left side of the second column of blocks and the top point with the top of the second row of blocks.

67 Save in Sketchbook. Save the project.

Tips and Tricks:

- Gather blocks to set into the Layer 2 blocks. Select a block, place the cursor *in the center* of any of the Layer 2 blocks, and click to set. *Special Note:* Since there are two blocks in the center of the quilt, click the Adjust tool and then the center small block to select it. Move this block to the side momentarily so you can set a block into the large square on-point. Then reposition the smaller square. Check the locator positions to assure accurate placement.

- With this template, you can add or change border styles and sizes without disturbing the center layout. But you cannot change the size of the center rectangle of the quilt without disturbing the center layout.

- Blocks used in the example on this page are from the EQ4 Block Libraries:
  - 11 blocks from 5 Contemporary Applique, Music
  - Star Group II from 5 Contemporary Applique, Starry Night

- Three borders were added to the layout for the illustrated example on the next page: Borders 1 and 3 are Mitered style and 1.00 wide on all sides; Border 2 is Triangle Out style and 12.00 on all sides.

- Blocks used in the example on the next page are from the EQ4 Block Libraries:
  - "Four-Patch Variation 3" from 1 Classic Pieced, Simple Blocks

Step 66

Music Under the Stars

- "Bluebird on Branch" from 5 Contemporary Applique, Animals
- "Robin on Branch" from 5 Contemporary Applique, Animals
- "Butterfly III" from 5 Contemporary Applique, Animals (edited by rotating 45 degrees)
- "Celtic Patch 4" from 5 Contemporary Applique, Celtic Blocks
- "Posey and Butterfly" from 5 Contemporary Applique, Flowers (edited by rotating posey 45 degrees
- "Ann's Garden Wreath" from 5 Contemporary Applique, Garden Blocks
- "Bird on a Fence" from 5 Contemporary Applique, Garden Blocks
- "Sunflower Fence" from 5 Contemporary Applique, Garden Blocks
- "Tree of Life" from 5 Contemporary Applique, Garden Blocks
- "Watering Can" from 5 Contemporary Applique, Garden Blocks

In the Garden of the Temple Court

EQ4 Magic   133

Skewing to a Diamond Layout

Here is another quilt layout template that is quite fun and produces dramatic magical results that look a lot like they popped out of a kaleidoscope. It takes a bit of patience to set up this layout, but it's worth it.

The instructions given here are for a layout that will be used for *design purposes only*. You will not necessarily get accurate templates for producing a quilt if you print out patterns from this layout. However, if and when you decide to construct a quilt of this kind, there are instructions given in this book for drawing the block that *will* produce accurate templates. See: DRAWING A 45° DIAMOND BLOCK.

1 On the WORKTABLE menu, click Work on Block.

2 On the BLOCK menu, point to New Block, click EasyDraw.

3 With the blank block on the worktable, click the Color tab and color the block red.

4 Save in Sketchbook. Answer yes to the question box.

5 On the WORKTABLE menu, click Work on Quilt.

6 On the QUILT menu, point to New Quilt, click Country Set.

7 Click the Layout tab. Slide the bar to set 26 for Width and 26 for Height. *Or* you may highlight the number for Width and type in 26. Press the Tab key twice on your keyboard and type 26 for Height.

8 On the LIBRARIES menu, click Block Library. Double-click EQ Libraries if this book is not already open. Double-click 1 Classic Pieced, and click Eight-Point Stars.

9 Find the block called Diamond and click it. Click Copy. Click Close.

Trick:
If you click the 4-block display button, Diamond will be the upper right block. Rest

Step 2

Step 7

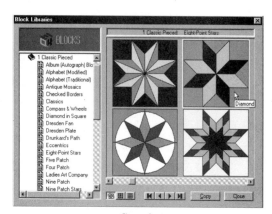

Step 9

Skewing to a Diamond Layout

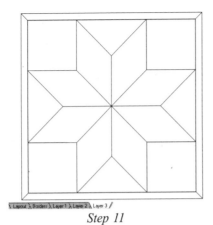

Step 11

Step 13

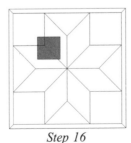

Step 16

your cursor on the block without clicking and the name of the block will appear.

10 Click the Layer 3 tab.

11 Click the Set tool. Click the Diamond block. Click, hold, and drag the cursor from the top-left corner of the quilt layout (do not include borders) down to the bottom-right corner to set the block. Release the mouse and the block will pop into the space. (A block set in Layer 3 will always appear as an outline with no color.)

🖑 **Note:**
If you do not have the Graph Pad on your quilt layout screen, click VIEW and click Graph Pad. You want to have a check mark next to Graph Pad on the menu.

12 Click the Adjust tool. Click the block you set in the quilt.

(Adjust tool)

13 On the Graph Pad, make the following adjustments:

- Horizontal location (top box on far left of Graph Pad): 0.00

- Vertical location (bottom box on far left of Graph Pad): 0.00

- Size width (top box in center of Graph Pad): 26.00

- Size height (bottom box in center of Graph Pad): 26.00

✎**Tip:**
This block was placed in Layer 3 because it will be an outline pattern for placing blank blocks in Layer 1. Layer 3 is usually the layer reserved for quilt patterns to position over a quilt top. Here we're using it for a guide. When we're ready to get rid of it as a guide, we can simply go into Layer 3, select the block with the Adjust tool, and press the Delete key on the keyboard.

14 Click the Layer 1 tab. Click the Set tool.

15 Click the blank block in the Sketchbook Blocks display. Click the right-arrow button to get the red colored version.

16 On the quilt worktable, click, hold, and drag a box any size. Release the mouse and

EQ4 Magic 135

Skewing to a Diamond Layout

the block will pop into the space.

17 Click the Adjust tool. Click the red block.

18 On the Graph Pad, make the following adjustments:

- Horizontal location: 0.00

- Vertical location: 0.00

- Size Width: 7.50

- Size Height: 7.50

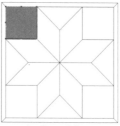

Step 18

19 Click the Set tool. Drag three more red boxes to fill in the remaining three corners. (The blocks will be specifically positioned in the next step.)

20 Click the Adjust tool. Click the first block that you sized and positioned in Step 18 as a reference block, move your cursor to a second block and then Ctrl+click. All the blocks in Layer 1 should be selected. Click the Same Size button on the far right of the Graph Pad. Click in a free space on the worktable away from the blocks to clear the cursor.

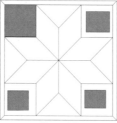

Step 19

 Trick:

You can select *all* the blocks in a layer by clicking one block (which may be used as a reference) and then holding down Ctrl as you click a second block. You will see all the blocks highlighted automatically with a light blue line. This will explain why all the blocks may be highlighted by mistake if you meant to press Shift, but pressed Ctrl instead.

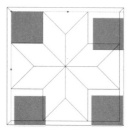

Step 20

21 On the Graph Pad, make the following adjustments to the respective blocks:

A) The upper-right corner block should have these locations:

- Horizontal: 18.50

- Vertical: 0.00

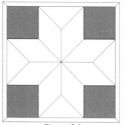

Step 21

B) The lower-left corner block should have these locations:

- Horizontal: 0.00

- Vertical: 18.50

Skewing to a Diamond Layout

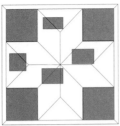

Step 22

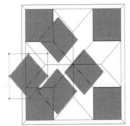

Step 23

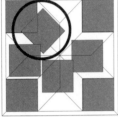

Step 24

Step 25

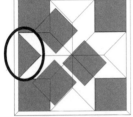

Steps 26-27

Step 28

Step 30

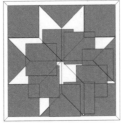

Step 31

C) The lower-right corner block should have these locations:

- Horizontal: 18.50
- Vertical: 18.50

22 Click the Set tool. Drag four more red boxes on the quilt layout.

23 Click the Adjust tool. Click one of the corner blocks for a reference block. Hold down the Shift key and click the four new blocks. Click the Same Size button. Clear the cursor.

24 Click one of these newly sized blocks. Click one of the arrows next to the Rotate tool on the Graph Pad. Type 45 in the box and the block will now be on-point.

25 Repeat step 24 for each of the other three newly sized blocks.

✎Tip:
You cannot multiple select these blocks and rotate them all together.

26 Click one of these rotated blocks and drag it to park in the setting triangle area on the side of the block. Park it carefully so the area is covered with the block. You may have to stretch it slightly to fit better.

27 With the block still selected, click the Clip tool on the far right of the Graph Pad to clip the block inside the border.

28 Repeat steps 26-27 for the other three blocks on-point. You will have to click the left clip tool button to clear the selection before clicking the right clip tool button each time.

29 Save in Sketchbook. Save the project.

30 Click the Set tool. Drag eight more red blocks.

↳ Note:
You may have to park some of these blocks off of the quilt worktable in the blank space to the right. Remember where they are sitting. They may disappear as you change from the Set tool to the Adjust tool, but if you click the

EQ4 Magic 137

space where you remember they are (with the Adjust tool), they will appear again.

31 Click the Adjust tool and click one of the corner blocks from step 12. Using this as the reference block, hold down the Shift key and click the eight new blocks. Click the Same Size tool button on the Graph Pad. Clear the cursor. (Note the illustration on the previous page.)

32 Click one of these new blocks to select it. Click an arrow of the Rotate tool on the Graph Pad and type in 45.

33 Repeat this step for the other seven blocks.

34 Click one of the newly rotated blocks and position your cursor on the bottom point of the block (it will be the bottom center spot on the marquee around the block). Click, hold, and drag the cursor upward and watch until the number in the Rotate tool box changes to 22, then release the mouse.

35 Adjust the width of the block using the box on the Graph Pad. Make the width 7.75 and the height 7.75.

36 With this block selected as the reference, hold down the Shift key and select the other blocks on-point. Click the Same Size button and all the blocks will be sized and skewed together. Clear the cursor.

37 Click one of these blocks and click an arrow of the Rotate tool on the Graph Pad. Type in 45. Drag the block to fill an appropriate space on the quilt.

38 Repeat this step one more time with another of the diamond blocks.

39 Select another diamond block and type in 0 for the Rotate tool. Drag into position.

40 Repeat this one time.

41 Select another diamond and type in 90 for the Rotation. Drag into position.

42 Repeat.

43 Select another diamond and type in 135 for the Rotation. Drag into position.

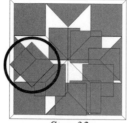

Step 32

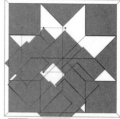

Step 33

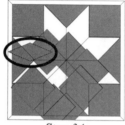

Step 34

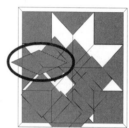

Step 35

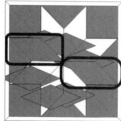

Steps 37-38

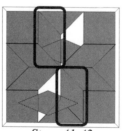

Steps 39-40

Steps 41-42

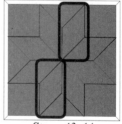

Steps 43-44

Skewing to a Diamond Layout

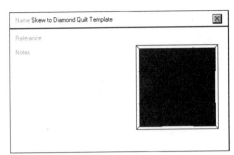

Step 48

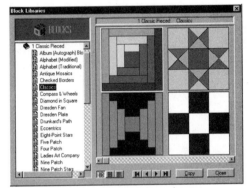

Steps 1-5

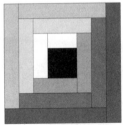

Step 3
(Log Cabin block)

Step 4
(Monkey Wrench block)

44 Repeat for the last block.

45 Adjust the stretch for any of the blocks in the star in order to get proper fit. Don't worry that the size may no longer be uniform. Remember that we are setting up this layout for designing purposes only, not for accurate templates.

46 Click the Layer 3 tab. With the Adjust tool enabled, click the Diamond block to select it. Press the Delete key. (You will not see a big difference in the quilt because you created a diamond with the blocks on Layer 1.) You may want to adjust Layer 1 again after deleting the Diamond in Layer 3.

47 Save in Sketchbook. Save the project.

48 Open the Sketchbook and click the Quilts tab. Click the Notecard for the quilt you just created. Name it "Skew to Diamond Quilt Template." Click the X to close the Notecard.

49 Click the X to close the Sketchbook. Save the project.

 Trick:
To use this layout template, save the file to different names as you design. Always keep this file clean for repetitive use.

Setting blocks into this quilt layout

1 On the LIBRARIES menu, click Block Library.

2 Double-click EQ Libraries if it is not already open, double-click 1 Classic Pieced, and click Classics.

3 The Log Cabin block is the first block on the display. Click the block to select it and click Copy.

4 Slide the slider bar all the way to the right to the last block, which is the Monkey Wrench block. Click to select it and click Copy.

5 Close the Library.

EQ4 Magic 139

Skewing to a Diamond Layout

6 Assuming you have the Skew to Diamond Quilt Template layout on the Quilt Worktable, click the Layer 1 tab and click the Set tool. Click the Log Cabin block on the Sketchbook blocks display.

7 Position your cursor *in the exact center of one of the blocks* on the quilt layout. Press Ctrl+click.

8 Like magic, your Log Cabin block should fill in all the blocks on the quilt. Click the Rotate tool on the right quilt toolbar and rotate blocks to get the coloring effect you like.

9 Add borders as you like. Do not change the size of the center rectangle of this quilt but you can add and delete borders as you continue to design without disturbing the center layout.

10 Save in Sketchbook and save the project whenever you find a quilt you like.

Use the Monkey Wrench block to design another fun quilt. Set the blocks as in step 7. Rotate to get the design you want.
Of course, you can try out any number of blocks for this exercise. Some will work better than others. You can get very complex looking designs. Remember that once you follow the directions below for getting accurate templates, you can actually get patterns from EQ4 to construct your favorite quilt designs. Often the blocks in the quilt may be foundation pieced. Considering you will need 4 square blocks, 4 half-square blocks, and 8 diamond blocks, the construction does not seem to be impossible, especially for foundation piecing!

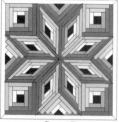
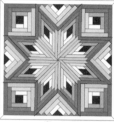

Step 7   *Step 8*

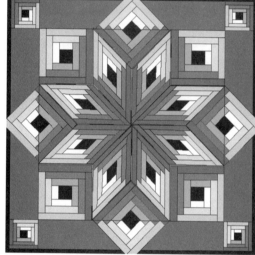

Step 9

Example of the quilt layout using the Monkey Wrench block

Making an Irregular Grid Quilt Layout

Step 2

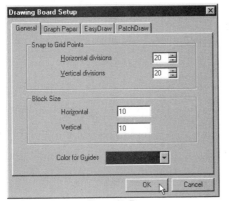

Steps 4-7

*Step 9
(Line Tool)*

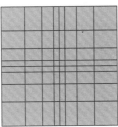

Steps 10-11

In EQ4, there are several quilt layouts automatically available for our designing use. Here, there are two different layouts described. Once you have these layouts set up, you can save the project file under the name "Irregular Grid Quilt Templates." Each time you want to create a different quilt file with the irregular grid, you can save the project under a different name. This layout will take some time to set up, but the end result is amazing!

1 On the WORKTABLE menu, click Work on Block.

2 On the BLOCK menu, point to New Block, click EasyDraw.

3 On the BLOCK menu, click Drawing Board Setup.

4 In the box for Snap to Grid Points, Horizontal divisions, type 20. Press the Tab key on your keyboard.

5 In the box for Vertical divisions, type 20. Press Tab.

6 In the Block Size, Horizontal, type 10. Press Tab.

7 In the Vertical size box type 10. Click OK.

🍂 Note:
If you don't see the rulers to the left and across the top of your document screen, click VIEW and Ruler.

8 Click the Snap to Grid tool. No other snap-to tools should be enabled. See: USING ADVANCED DRAWING FEATURES and CUSTOMIZING THE DRAWING TOOLBARS.

9 Click the Line tool.

10 Draw vertical lines from the top to the bottom of the block at 2", 3½", 4½", 5", 5½", 6½", and 8."

11 Draw horizontal lines from left to right on the block at 2", 3½", 4½", 5", 5½", 6½", and 8."

EQ4 Magic 141

12 Click the Color tab. Click the Spray Can tool.

13 Click any patch on the block to highlight the entire block.

14 Click a light neutral color on the Color Palette to color the entire block at once.

15 Save in Sketchbook. Save the project.

16 Click View Sketchbook. Click the Blocks tab and click the new block. Click Notecard and name the block "Template 1 for Irregular Grid." Click the X to close the Notecard. Click the X to close the Sketchbook.

17 Save the project.

You will need one more block to set up the Irregular Grid quilt layout.

18 On the BLOCK menu, point to New Block, click Easy Draw.

19 Click the Color tab. Color the square any color that contrasts with the template layout block you drew previously (therefore, use a dark color such as red).

20 Save in Sketchbook. Answer Yes in the question box. Save the project.

Setting up the Irregular Grid 1 Quilt Layout Template

1 On the WORKTABLE menu, click Work on Quilt.

2 On the QUILT menu, point to New Quilt, click Country Set.

3 Click the Layout tab. Slide the bar to set 40 for Width and 40 for Height. *Or* you may highlight the number for Width and type in 40. Press the Tab key twice on your keyboard and type 40 for Height.

4 Click the Borders tab. To not have a border at this time, in Size of Border, drag the sliding bars to the far left to set 0.00 for Left, Top, Right, and Bottom.

Step 12
(Spray Can tool)

Step 15

(Save in   (Save -
Sketchbook)   project)

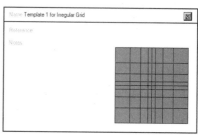

Step 16

Step 2

Step 3

Step 4

Making an Irregular Grid Quilt Layout

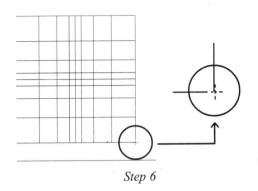

Step 6

*Step 7
(Adjust tool)*

Step 8

Making an Irregular Grid Quilt Layout

Trick:
You can change the Borders setup of your quilt after you have designed the center in Country Set layout and the center will adjust automatically.

5   Click the Layer 3 tab.

6   Click the Set tool. Click your "Template 1" block in the Sketchbook Blocks display. Click, hold, and drag the cursor from the top-left corner of the quilt layout down to the bottom-right corner to set the block. Release the mouse and the block will pop into the space. (A block set in Layer 3 will always appear as an outline with no color.)

Note:
If you do not have the Graph Pad on your quilt layout screen, click VIEW and click Graph Pad. You want to have a check mark next to Graph Pad on the menu.

7   Click the Adjust tool. Click the block you set in the quilt.

8   On the Graph Pad, make the following adjustments:

- Horizontal location (top box on far left of Graph Pad): 0.00

- Vertical location (bottom box on far left of Graph Pad): 0.00

- Size width (top box in center of Graph Pad): 40.00

- Size height (bottom box in center of Graph Pad): 40.00

9   Save in Sketchbook. Save the project.

Tip:
This block was placed in Layer 3 because it will be an outline pattern for placing blank blocks in Layer 1. Layer 3 is usually the layer reserved for quilt patterns to position over a quilt top. Here we're using it for a guide. When we're ready to get rid of it as a guide, we can simply go into Layer 3, select the block with the Adjust tool, and press the Delete key on the keyboard.

10   Click the Layer 1 tab. Click the Set tool.

EQ4 Magic   143

11 Click the blank block in the Sketchbook Blocks display. Click the right-arrow button to get the dark colored version.

12 Click, hold, and drag 8 dark blocks anywhere on the quilt layout.

13 Click the Adjust tool. Click one of the blocks you just set.

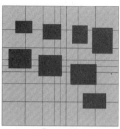

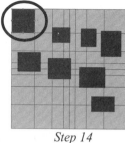

Step 12   *Step 14*

14 On the Graph Pad, make the following adjustments:

- Horizontal location: 0.00

- Vertical location: 0.00

- Size width: 8.00

- Size height: 8.00

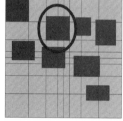

(Same size tool)

Step 15

15 With the block still selected, hold down the Shift key on your keyboard as you click one other block. Release the Shift key. Click the Same Size button on the Graph Pad.

16 Click in a free space on the worktable away from the blocks to clear the cursor.

17 Click the newly-sized block. Click, hold, and drag it to the top-right corner of the layout. (Do not worry about perfect positioning for this block yet. We'll clean it up later.)

18 Click an unsized blank block.

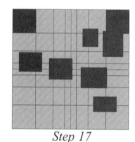

Step 17

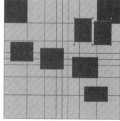

Result of Steps 19-20

19 On the Graph Pad, make the following size adjustments (again, the position will be set later):

- Size width: 6.00

- Size height: 8.00

20 With the block still selected, hold down the Shift key as you click another block. Release the Shift key. Click the Same Size button. Clear the cursor.

21 Click one of the 6x8 blocks. Click, hold, and drag it to the right of the 8x8 block in the upper-left corner. (Use the template in Layer 3 as your guide. Exact positioning is not important yet.)

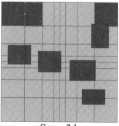

Step 21

Making an Irregular Grid Quilt Layout

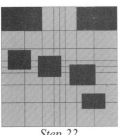

Step 22

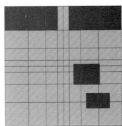

Step 24

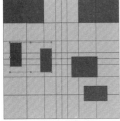

Step 25

Step 26

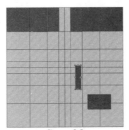

Step 28

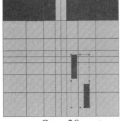

Step 29

Step 30

22 Click the second 6x8 block. Click, hold, and drag it to the left of the 8x8 block in the upper-right corner.

23 Click another unsized blank block.

24 On the Graph Pad, make the following size adjustments (the position will be set later):

- Size width: 4.00
- Size height: 8.00

25 With the block still selected, hold down the Shift key as you click another block. Release the Shift key. Click the Same Size button. Clear the cursor.

26 Click, hold, and drag each of these 4x8 blocks in position on the top row of the grid. (You do not have to have exact positioning. You are filling in the spaces on the top row of your layout template block that you set in Layer 3.)

27 Click one of the last two unsized blank blocks.

28 On the Graph Pad, make the following size adjustments (the position will be set later):

- Size width: 2.00
- Size height: 8.00

29 With the block still selected, hold down the Shift key as you click the last block. Release the Shift key. Click the Same Size button. Clear the cursor.

30 Click, hold, and drag these two blocks in the center of the top row.

Now we will start to position these blocks in the top row accurately. Here starts the magic!

31 Using the Adjust tool, click to select the top left block, which was positioned accurately earlier. Hold the Shift key as you select the rest of the blocks in the top row. Release the Shift key once all the blocks have been selected.

↳ Note:

It is important to click the block that has already been adjusted first. Then click the

EQ4 Magic **145**

Making an Irregular Grid Quilt Layout

block that is to be aligned the same.

32 On the Graph Pad, click the Align button with the horizontal line over two squares. This will bring all the selected blocks into alignment with the top of the first block selected. (The Vertical locator box will read 0.00 for each of these blocks.) Clear the cursor.

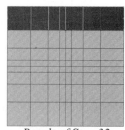

Step 32   *Result of Step 32*

You now need to select and align each block horizontally with the position locator on the left side of the Graph Pad.

Use the Graph Pad to complete Step 33

33 As you select each of these blocks in the top row, the lower box number (vertical) should be 0.00. From left to right, as you adjust the position of each block in the row, the upper box number (horizontal) should be 0.00, 8.00, 14.00, 18.00, 20.00, 22.00, 26.00, and 32.00.

34 Save in Sketchbook. Save the project.

35 Set up the left column of the block in the same way you did the first row. The size for the blocks are all 8.00 wide. The height measurements will be 8, 6, 4, and 2 (as you go down the column). You will need 2 blocks of each size. Remember to use the Same Size tool.

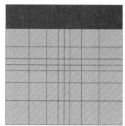

Step 33

✎Tip:
If you try to set a block outline that is too small, it will not appear on the quilt layout. To fix this, outline a larger block area to set the block and resize it with the Adjust tool.

36 When you have roughly positioned this vertical column of blocks on the left, select them all. Be sure to click your reference block (the top-left block) first. Hold down the Shift key as you click the other blocks in the column. Release the Shift key. Click the Align to Left button (the tool has a vertical line to the left of two squares) on the Graph Pad.

Step 36

37 Again, you can fine tune with the position locators. For this column, the upper number (horizontal) for each block should be 0.00. The lower numbers (vertical)

Result of Steps 35-37

Making an Irregular Grid Quilt Layout

should be, from top to bottom of the column, 0.00, 8.00, 14.00, 18.00, 20.00, 22.00, 26.00, and 32.00.

38 Save in Sketchbook. Save the project.

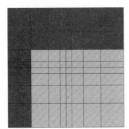

Result of Steps 39-40

39 Set the second horizontal row of blocks as you did for the first row. Note that the block sizes for this row need to be 6.00 high and 8.00, 6.00, 4.00, and 2.00 wide. You need to set only 7 blocks, since you have the first block of this row already in position in the left column.

40 Click the Adjust tool and align the tops of the blocks in this second row as you did in step 31.

41 Continue filling in the grid (overlapping the block in Layer 3). I would recommend, for efficiency, setting blocks in one horizontal row at a time. Adjust vertical positioning by aligning the tops of all the blocks as each row is set.

♣ Note:
You may have to park some of these blocks off of the quilt worktable in the blank space to the right. Remember where they are sitting. They may disappear as you change from the Set tool to the Adjust tool, but if you click the space where you remember they are (with the Adjust tool), they will appear again.

42 When you have finished setting the blocks for the entire quilt, you can adjust positioning by aligning columns to the left as you did in step 36.

 Trick:
You set up your perfect positioning with the blocks set in the top row and the left side column. Use those blocks as your reference by selecting one of them first, then with the Shift key held down, select the rest of the blocks in the row or column and click on the appropriate Alignment tool.

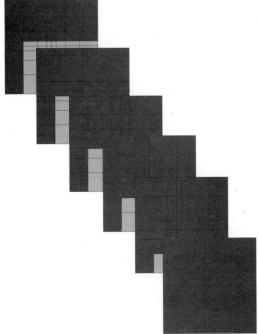

Result of Step 41-42

43 Save in Sketchbook. Save the project.

EQ4 Magic 147

44 Click View Sketchbook. Click the Quilts tab. Click the right arrow button to see the last saved quilt. Click Notecard. Type in a name for the quilt layout, such as "Irregular Grid Layout," and record any comments. Click the X to close the Notecard. Click the X to close the Sketchbook.

45 Save the project.

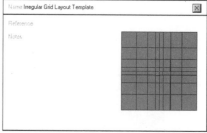

Step 44

Playing with the Irregular Grid Quilt Layout

Now we're ready for the greatest magic trick! Hold onto your magician's top hat!

1 On the LIBRARIES menu, click Block Library. Double-click EQ Libraries if this book is not already open. Double-click 1 Classic Pieced, and click Simple Blocks. (You may have to scroll down to find the Simple Blocks page. It is an alphabetical listing.)

2 Find these blocks: Half Square Triangle, Diagonal Strips, Diamond in the Square, and Attic Window. Click each block and click Copy. Click Close.

Trick:
Rest your cursor on the block without clicking and the name of the block will appear.

3 With the Irregular Grid Layout quilt on Layer 1, click the Set tool.

4 Click the Diamond in the Square block in the Sketchbook Blocks display.

5 Position your cursor **in the center** of one of the blocks on the quilt. Hold down the Ctrl key on your keyboard and click. All your blocks will be filled with the Diamond in the Square block. Your quilt should look like all the blocks are falling into a hole in the center. (Isn't that an amazing magic trick?)

Step 2
(Half Square Triangle)

Step 2
(Diagonal Strips)

Step 2
(Diamond in the Square)

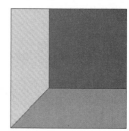

Step 2
(Attic Window)

Step 5
(Using the Diamond in the Square block)

6 Click another block in the Sketchbook Blocks display and repeat step 5. See what a difference that makes!

7 Do some experimenting. Rotate the blocks. Try rotating them in quadrants, meaning, rotate all the blocks in the upper right quarter of the quilt once, the blocks in the lower right quarter twice, and the lower left quarter three times.

8 Go back into the Block Library and find more blocks to use. I would caution that you choose simple blocks with few pieces for best visual effect.

9 Don't forget to Save in Sketchbook and Save the project as you explore the possibilities and find nifty quilts to amaze your friends.

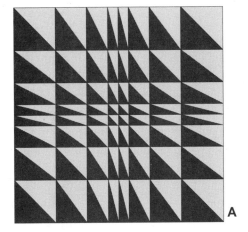

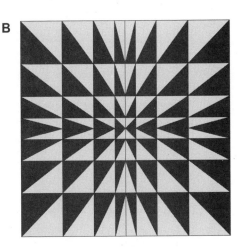

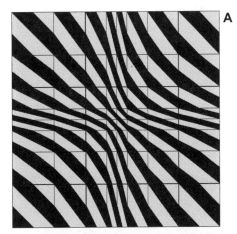

A - Examples of Step 6
B - Examples of Step 7

EQ4 Magic 149

Another Irregular Grid

If you liked the irregular grid that had blocks falling into a hole in the center, perhaps you'd also like this one with a reverse effect. Now you can design a quilt that looks like it has a basketball under the center of it – on purpose! Abracadabra. Here we go!

1   On the WORKTABLE menu, click Work on block.

2   On the BLOCK menu, point to New Block, click EasyDraw.

3   Keep the same drawing board set-up that you used for the "Template 1 for Irregular Grid" block. (Be sure you have Rulers showing.)

4   Draw your vertical lines at ½", 1½", 3", 5", 7",8½", and 9½."

5   Draw your horizontal lines at ½", 1½", 3", 5", 7", 8½", and 9½."

6   Click the Color tab. Color all the sections in a neutral/light color. Save in Sketchbook.

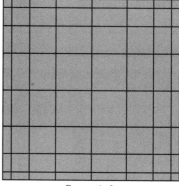

Steps 4-6

7   Click View Sketchbook. Click the Blocks tab and select this block. Click Notecard. Name the block "Irregular Grid Template 2." Click the X to Close the Notecard. Click the X to Close the Sketchbook.

8   Save the project.

Setting up the Irregular Grid 2 Quilt Layout

1   Use the "Irregular Grid Template 2" as you follow the same instructions as for Irregular Grid 1 Quilt Layout Template. You will need to make the following adjustments: In Layer 1, the position locations for the top row of blocks are 2.00, 6.00, 12.00, 20.00, 28.00, 34.00, and 38.00 for the upper box numbers (horizontal) and 0.00 for the lower box number (vertical).

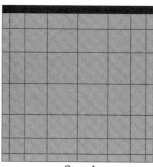

Step 1

Making an Irregular Grid Quilt Layout

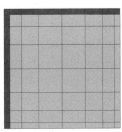

Step 2

Step 3

2 For the left column of blocks, the position locations are 0.00 for the upper box number (horizontal) and 2.00, 6.00, 12.00, 20.00, 28.00, 34.00, and 38.00 for the lower box numbers (vertical).

✎**Tip:**
The blank block sizes here are the same as for Irregular Grid 1. When you use the Graph Pad to size these blocks, remember that you will be using only the whole numbers 2, 4, 6, and 8. Only the placement of these blocks in Irregular Grid 2 is different. Use the template block set in Layer 3 as your guide for blank block placement in Layer 1.

3 Proceed to set blank blocks into this grid as you did with the Irregular Grid 1 instructions. Save in Sketchbook. Save the project.

4 Click View Sketchbook. Click the right arrow to see the last quilt. Click Notecard. Name the quilt layout "Irregular Grid 2 Quilt Template" and make any noteworthy comments. Click the X to Close the Notecard. Click X to Close the Sketchbook.

5 Save the project.

6 You will be ready once more for the magic show of optical illusions when you set your blocks into the quilt.

Step 6
Using the Diamond in the Square block (compare this quilt with the quilt made with the grid layout 1)

Making an Irregular Grid Quilt Layout

EQ4 Magic **151**

Making Grandmother's Flower Garden

We can design quilts with polygons other than squares, rectangles, and diamonds by drawing motifs in PatchDraw and setting these interlocking shapes in Country Set or in Layer 2 of any other quilt layout.

Drawing the flower motif unit

1   On the WORKTABLE menu, click Work on Block.

2   On the BLOCK menu, point to New Block, click PatchDraw.

3   Click the BLOCK menu and click Drawing Board Setup.

4   On the General tab, type 6 for Snap to Grid Points, Horizontal divisions. Press the Tab key on your keyboard.

5   Type 6 for Vertical divisions. Press Tab.

6   Type 9 for Block Size, Horizontal. Press Tab.

7   Type 9 for Block Size, Vertical.

8   Click the Graph Paper tab.

9   For the Number of Divisions, type 6 for Horizontal. Press Tab. Type 6 for Vertical.

10   Under Options, click the down arrow by the Style box. Click Graph paper lines. Click OK.

11   Click the dark arrow in the corner of the Polygon tool to get the pop-out display of shapes. Click the hexagon.

12   Click, hold, and drag to connect any two horizontal corners of the graph paper lines. (Be sure you keep the top line of the hexagon in a perfect horizontal orientation.) Release the mouse. (Note illustration.)

Trick:
You may erase this hexagon and start again by clicking EDIT and Undo. Another way to do this is to press Ctrl+Z.

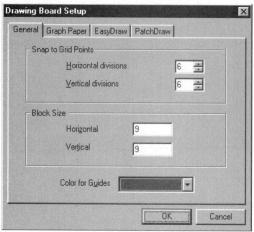

Steps 3-7

Steps 8-10

Step 11

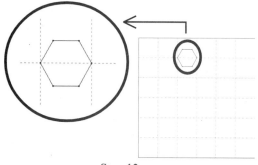

Step 12

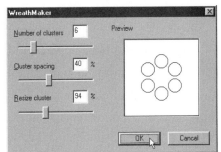

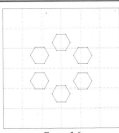

Step 16

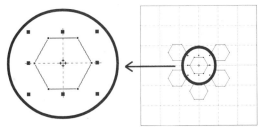

Step 19

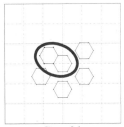

Step 21   *Step 22*

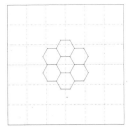

Step 24

13 Click the Select tool.

14 Click the hexagon to select it.

15 On the BLOCK menu, click Wreathmaker.

16 Click, hold and drag the slide on each slider bar to change the numbers in the boxes. Make these settings: Number of clusters 6; Cluster spacing 40; Resize cluster 94. Click OK.

Trick:
You can also change the settings by typing in the numbers and pressing Tab twice to advance to the next number.

17 Click in a free space on the worktable away from the wreath to clear the cursor.

18 Have all snap-to tools disenabled at this time. See: USING ADVANCED DRAWING FEATURES and CUSTOMIZING THE DRAWING TOOLBARS.

19 Click one hexagon. Click, hold, and drag the hexagon so it's exactly over the center of the graph paper lines in the middle of the worktable. (Note illustration.)

20 Click the Auto Align Similar Lines tool. (All other snap-to tools should still remain disenabled.)

21 Click another hexagon. Click, hold, and drag this hexagon so it aligns exactly with one side of the first hexagon.

22 Repeat this step with the other hexagons. Each hexagon should align with a different side of the first hexagon to start to form the first ring around the center.

23 Click one hexagon. Press Ctrl+C to copy the shape. Press Ctrl+V to paste the copied hexagon onto your drawing board.

24 Click, hold, and drag this last hexagon into position to complete the first ring around the center.

25 Save in Sketchbook. Save the project.

EQ4 Magic   153

26 Paste (Ctrl+V) 12 more hexagons onto your drawing board.

27 Click, hold, and drag each of the 12 new hexagons around the first ring to form the second ring.

28 Save in Sketchbook. Save the project.

29 Paste 18 more hexagons on the worktable. (You may not want to paste all 18 hexagons at the same time, it may be become confusing. Instead you can paste and set 6 hexagons three times.)

30 Click, hold, and drag the new hexagons around the second ring to form the third ring.

31 Save to the Sketchbook and Save the project file.

32 With the Select tool, click the outline of the block and press the Delete key on your keyboard.

33 Click the Color tab. Color your block. (Traditionally the outer row of hexagons would be colored green to indicate the garden path between the flowers and the center hexagon would be yellow for the flower center. Often the flowers themselves would be multi-colors, and those can be colored or changed on the quilt layout.)

34 Save in Sketchbook. Save the project.

35 Click View Sketchbook, click the Blocks tab, and click the last block in the Sketchbook. Click Notecard.

36 Name this block "Grandmother's Flower Garden." Type in any other notes you may want to record. Click the X to close the Notecard. Click the X to close the Sketchbook.

37 Save the project.

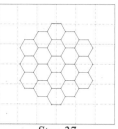

Step 27

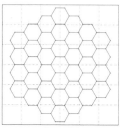

Step 30

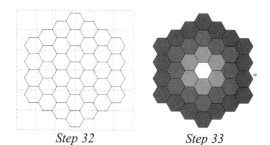

Step 32   *Step 33*

Name Grandmother's Flower Garden

Reference

Notes

Step 36

Making Grandmother's Flower Garden

Step 3

(*Plain Block tool*)

Step 5

Step 6

Step 8

Laying out the Grandmother's Flower Garden Quilt - Version 1

The Grandmother's Flower Garden blocks will appear to be on point in this version of the quilt layout.

1   On the WORKTABLE menu, click Work on Quilt.

2   On the QUILT menu, point to New Quilt, click Country Set.

3   Click the Layout tab. Slide the bar to set 42 for Width and 44 for Height *Or* you may highlight the number for Width and type in 42. Press the Tab key twice on your keyboard and type 44 for Height.

4   Click the Layer 1 tab.

✎ Note:

If you do not have the Graph Pad on your quilt layout screen, click VIEW and click Graph Pad. You want to have a check mark next to Graph Pad on the menu.

Because the Grandmother's Flower Garden quilt usually has an irregular edge, we'll set a plain block as a base to the quilt. This is so that you can color a background for your quilt.

5   Click the Plain block tool and select a neutral solid color from the color palette.

6   Click, hold, and drag the cursor from the top-left corner of the quilt to the bottom-right corner. Release the cursor and the quilt layout will fill with color.

7   Click the Adjust tool. Click the plain block you set in the quilt

8   On the Graph Pad, make the following adjustments:

- Horizontal location (top box on far left of Graph Pad): 0.00

- Vertical location (bottom box on far left of Graph Pad): 0.00

- Size width (top box in center of Graph Pad): 42.00

EQ4 Magic   155

- Size height (bottom box in center of Graph Pad): 44.00

9 Click the Layer 2 tab. (We will be setting the Grandmother's Flower Garden blocks in Layer 2 because we don't want to disturb the plain block in Layer 1.)

10 Click the Set tool. Click the Grandmother's Flower Garden block. Find the colored version by clicking the right-arrow button.

11 Click, hold, and drag a box any size onto the quilt layout.

12 Click the Adjust tool. Click the block you just set.

13 On the Graph Pad make the following size adjustments:

- Width: 9.00
- Height: 9.00

14 Click the Set tool. Drag five more blocks onto the quilt layout. (Do not worry about the size of these blocks yet.)

15 Click the Adjust tool. Click the first block you sized in step 13. Hold down the Shift key as you click the other 5 blocks. Release the Shift key. Click the Same Size button on the far-right of the Graph Pad.

16 Click in a free space on the worktable away from the blocks to clear the cursor.

17 Click, hold, and drag one block to the bottom-left corner of the quilt layout so the edges of the box outlining the block fit into the corner. (Note illustration.)

18 Click, hold, and drag the next block to the right side of the first block but overlap one vertical row of hexagons. (If you colored this last ring the traditional green, you will be overlapping three green hexagons from one block onto three green hexagons from the first block. Don't be concerned which block does the overlapping. It doesn't matter.)

Step 11

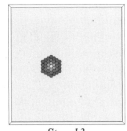
Step 13

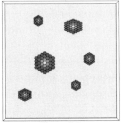
Step 14

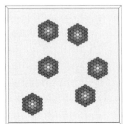
Step 15

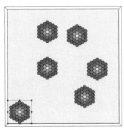
Step 17

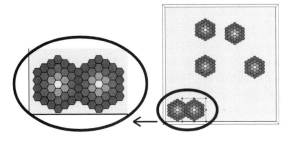
Step 18

Step 19

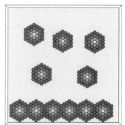
Step 21

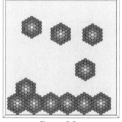
Step 22

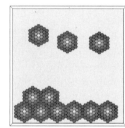
Step 23

Step 25

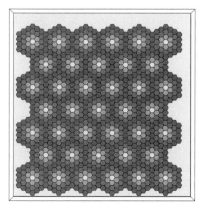
Step 26

19 Continue placing blocks across the quilt. (You will have room for six.)

20 Save in Sketchbook. Save the project.

21 Set and size 5 more blocks.

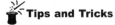**Trick:**
Size the blocks by using a block from the first row as your master sizing block.

22 Drag the first block in the second row between the first two blocks from the first row. You will have a zig-zag edge to the quilt. It will appear as though every flower block has only 1 outside ring. Therefore, several flower blocks will share the same outside ring by overlapping.

23 Repeat Step 22 and add the next block from Step 21 between blocks 2 and 3 from the first row. Again, one vertical row of hexagons will overlap.

24 Save in Sketchbook. Save the project (after the addition of each row).

25 Finish dragging the remaining 3 blocks from Step 21 into position.

26 Continue to set and size the blocks. Then position in the rows until the quilt looks like the illustration. You will have room to position seven rows horizontally on the layout in this example.

27 Save once more in Sketchbook and Save the project.

28 Click View Sketchbook. Click the Quilts tab. Click the last quilt in the Sketchbook (click the far-right arrow to see the last quilt). Click Notecard. Name this quilt "Grandmother's Flower Garden Version 1." Click X to close the Notecard. Click X to close the Sketchbook.

29 Save the project.

Tips and Tricks

• **You cannot change the size of the center rectangle of the quilt without disturbing the center layout. (You can change or add border styles without distrubing the center layout.)**

EQ4 Magic **157**

- You may want to play with the coloring of the background block or set the Grandmother's Flower Garden blocks more randomly so the background color peeks through. Go to Layer 1 to change the color of the background. Click the Paintbrush tool and select the color. Click any exposed area of the background block and the color will change.

Laying out the Grandmother's Flower Garden Quilt - Version 2

The Grandmother's Flower Garden blocks will appear to be straight set in this version of the quilt layout.

1 On the WORKTABLE menu, click Work on Quilt.

2 On the QUILT menu, point to New Quilt, click Country Set.

3 Click the Layout tab. Slide the bar to set 43 for Width and 42 for Height *Or* you may highlight the number for Width and type in 43. Press the Tab key twice on your keyboard and type 42 for Height.

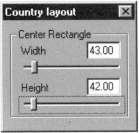

Step 3

4 Click the Layer 1 tab.

ℕ Note:

If you do not have the Graph Pad on your quilt layout screen, click VIEW and click Graph Pad. You want to have a check mark next to Graph Pad on the menu.

Because the Grandmother's Flower Garden quilt usually has an irregular edge, we'll set a plain block as a base to the quilt. This is so that you can color a background for your quilt.

5 Click the Plain block tool and select a neutral solid color from the color palette.

(Plain Block tool)

Step 5

6 Click, hold, and drag the cursor from the top-left corner of the quilt to the bottom right corner. Release the cursor and the quilt layout will fill with color.

7 Click the Adjust tool. Click the plain block you set in the quilt

8 On the Graph Pad, make the following adjustments:

- Horizontal location (top box on far left of Graph Pad): 0.00

Step 6

Making Grandmother's Flower Garden

Step 8

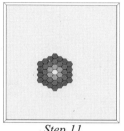

Step 11

Step 13

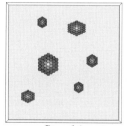

Step 14

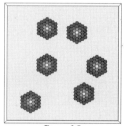

Step 15

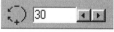

Step 17

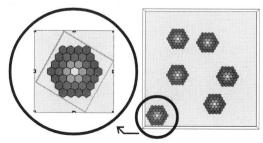

Steps 17-19

- Vertical location (bottom box on far left of Graph Pad): 0.00

- Size width (top box in center of Graph Pad): 43.00

- Size height (bottom box in center of Graph Pad): 42.00

9 Click the Layer 2 tab. (We will be setting the Grandmother's Flower Garden blocks in Layer 2 because we don't want to disturb the plain block in Layer 1.)

10 Click the Set tool. Click the Grandmother's Flower Garden block. Find the colored version by clicking the right-arrow button.

11 Click, hold, and drag a box any size onto the quilt layout.

12 Click the Adjust tool. Click the block you just set.

13 On the Graph Pad make the following size adjustments:

- Width: 9.00

- Height: 9.00

14 Click the Set tool. Drag six more blocks onto the quilt layout. (Do not worry about the size of these blocks yet.)

15 Click the Adjust tool. Click the first block you sized in step 13. Hold down the Shift key as you click the other 6 blocks. Release the Shift key. Click the Same Size button on the far-right of the Graph Pad.

16 Click in a free space on the worktable away from the blocks to clear the cursor.

17 Click one of the blocks. Click an arrow next to the Rotate box on the Graph Pad. Type 30.

18 Repeat step 17 for the other 6 blocks.

19 Click, hold, and drag one block to the bottom-left corner of the quilt layout so the edges of the box outlining the block fit into the corner. (Note illustration.)

EQ4 Magic 159

Making Grandmother's Flower Garden

20 Place the next block to the side of the first block but overlap one row of hexagons.

21 Continue placing blocks across the quilt. You should have room for seven in a zig-zag row.

22 Save to the Sketchbook. Save the project.

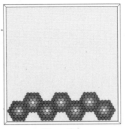
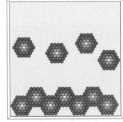

Step 21   *Steps 23-24*

23 Set 4 more blocks. Size one block to 9 inches square as you did before. Press Shift and click the other blocks to do a multiple select. Click the Same Size button on the Graph Pad.

24 Rotate each block 30 degrees, as you did in Step 17 (or 18).

Note:
You cannot multiple select and rotate these blocks all together. Neither can you select a rotated block and use it as the master size block to resize other blocks. You will not get the correct size. You may want to keep a sized but unrotated block off to the side of your worktable for future reference use.

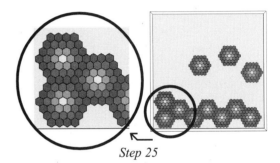

Step 25

25 Drag the first block in the second row up between the first two blocks from the first row. (Note illustration.) It will appear as though every flower block has only 1 out-side ring. Therefore, several flower blocks will share the same outside ring.

26 Repeat step 25 for the remaining 3 blocks.

27 Save in Sketchbook and Save the project after the addition of each row.

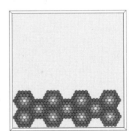

Step 26

28 Continue setting, sizing, rotating, and placing blocks. You should have room to position seven rows vertically as shown in the illustration.

29 Save in Sketchbook and Save the project.

30 Click View Sketchbook. Click the Quilts tab. Click the last quilt in the Sketchbook. Click Notecard. Name this quilt "Grandmother's Flower Garden Version 2." Click the X to close the Notecard. Click the X to close the Sketchbook.

31 Save the project.

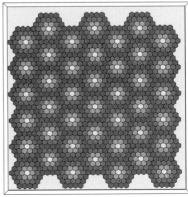

Step 28

Making Grandmother's Flower Garden

Chapter 5
Tips and Tricks

Chapter 5
Tips and Tricks

Right-Clicking

Right-click on
EasyDraw
worktable

Right-click on
PatchDraw
worktable

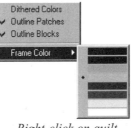

Right-click on quilt
worktable

Right-click on solid
color palette

Right-click on fabric
palette

When in doubt, right-click.

QUESTION

What does right-click do?

ANSWER

1   It brings out some useful pop-up menus as shortcuts.

2   For example, right- click on an EasyDraw worktable and the pop-up menu will offer Convert to Guides, Clear Guides, Grid Setup, and tools for Editing, Symmetry, Resizing, and Rotating. In PatchDraw, add Wreathmaker to that list.

3   Right-click on a quilt worktable and the pop-up menu will offer options for Outlining Blocks, Outlining Patches, and choosing the color of the selection frame.

4   Right-click on the solid color palette and you can add colors, sort them, make colors, and change the display.

5   Right-click on the fabric palette and you can change colorways, sort the fabrics, and change the display.

6   If you have enabled Customizing the Drawing Toolbars through FILE, Preferences, Drawing Options, a right-click on any button on the right toolbar on a block worktable will open the pop-up display of tools you can drag to add to your toolbar in EasyDraw and in PatchDraw.

Right-Clicking

Customize your toolbar in
EasyDraw

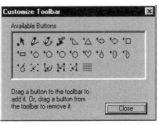

Customize your toolbar in
PatchDraw

EQ4 Magic   163

Learning Tricks of the Trade

You don't have to be a magician to have a bag of magic tricks. I have learned as I demonstrate EQ4 that I take it for granted some of the shortcuts that I use frequently. Since I have been asked, "How did you do that?" I will list some of the shortcuts for you. The hotkeys (keyboard shortcuts), when there are any, are listed next to the menu commands in the extended or pop-up menus in EQ4. All of these hotkey combinations may be familiar to Windows users – you just have to realize you can use them in EQ4 too!

Find which of these "shortcuts" works best for you. It all depends on how you use the combination of your mouse and keyboard.

Listed under each of the following categories are different ways to complete a function. They are not step-by-step instructions. **Each number indicates another way to perform the function.**

There's more than one way to:

Copy and Paste

1   On the VIEW menu, click Edit Tools to place a check by it. Three buttons for Cut, Copy, and Paste, that are familiar to Windows users, will appear on your left tool bar. The buttons are grayed out when something is not selected. But once you have a shape or line selected, you can click the Copy and Paste buttons.

2   To copy, press Ctrl+C. To paste, press Ctrl+V.

3   On the drawing boards, use the Select tool, Symmetry menu (accessed by clicking the dark square in the corner of the Select tool) to Clone by clicking the line and clicking the word Clone. This is the best short cut to use for copying and pasting when you also want to rotate the unit.

4   On the EDIT menu, click Copy or Paste once you have a line or shape selected from a drawing board.

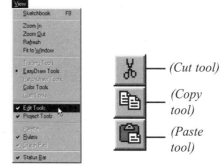

(Cut tool)
(Copy tool)
(Paste tool)

Copy and Paste 1

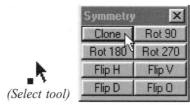

(Select tool)

Copy and Paste 3

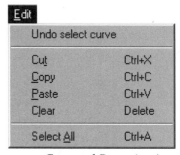

Copy and Paste 4

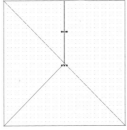

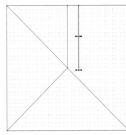

Copy and Paste 6

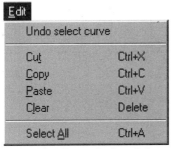

Undo, Cut or Delete 3-5

(Adjust tool)
Undo, Cut or Delete 7

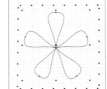

(Select tool) *(For emphasis, the marquee has been darkened and enlarged)*

Select All 2

5 You can use these copy and paste tools to transfer text between Notecards or from a Notecard to a word processor document.

6 You can copy a shape or figure from one EasyDraw drawing board and paste it to another EasyDraw drawing board, from one PatchDraw drawing board to another PatchDraw drawing board, or from either of the above to the appropriate layer of the Overlaid block drawing board.

Undo, Cut or Delete

1 Press Ctrl+Z up to 10 times to delete current and successive past drawing lines, colors, and block sets.

2 Press Ctrl+X to cut. This deletes the selected line or shape from its position and places it on the clipboard. You may then paste it elsewhere. This is different from Delete. Only one item stays on the clipboard at a time. When you select something else to cut, the first item disappears.

3 On the EDIT menu, click Cut to delete the item. Cutting the segment puts it on your clipboard for pasting later.

4 On the EDIT menu, click Clear to delete.

5 On the EDIT menu, click Undo.

6 On the drawing boards, click the Select tool to select the line or shape. Then press the Delete key on your keyboard.

7 On the quilt worktable, click the Adjust tool, click a block to select it, and press the Delete key.

Select All

1 On the Block Worktable, press Ctrl+A. If you're in PatchDraw, this will also select the outside border of the block. You can choose to deselect this border by holding down Shift and clicking the border.

2 Click the Select tool and drag a box (marquee) around all the lines or shapes you want to select.

EQ4 Magic **165**

Change between the (Line or Arc or Bezier) drawing tool and Edit tool

1   Click the appropriate tool button on the right tool bar.

2   Press the Spacebar on your keyboard to toggle between the two. This will work if you are going between only these two tools.

Open a File

1   Open a file from EQ4's opening screen.

2   On the FILE menu, click Open.

3   Press Ctrl+O.

4   Click the Open a Project button near the top of the left toolbar.

Start a New File

1   Name a new file from the opening screen of the program.

2   Click Cancel on the opening screen of the program and work on the drawing and quilt worktables. When you're ready to save your project, on the FILE menu, click Save As and name your project file. *Beware that you will now be saving your file to your My Documents folder unless you change your directory or folder for where to place this EQ4 project file.*

3   Press Ctrl+N.

4   Click the Create a New Project button at the top of the left toolbar.

Save in Sketchbook

1   Click the Save in Sketchbook button on the left toolbar.

2   On the BLOCK menu, click Save in Sketchbook.

3   On the QUILT menu, click Save in Sketchbook.

Save a File that Has Been Named

1   Click the Save in Sketchbook button on the left toolbar. Then click the Save button (a

Open a File 1

[(Open a Project (Ctrl+O)]
Open a File 4

Start a New File 1

(Create a New Project)
Start a New File 4

(Save in Sketchbook)
Save in Sketchbook 1

Save in Sketchbook 2   *Save in Sketchbook 3*

[Save (Ctrl+S)]
Save a File that
Has Been Named 1

Save a File that Has Been Named 3

(View Sketchbook) Open the Sketchbook 1

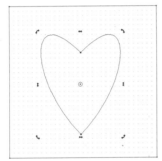

Rotate Drawing Lines or Shapes 1

Rotate Drawing Lines or Shapes 2

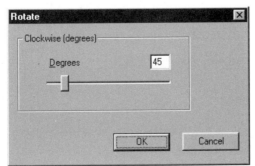

Rotate Drawing Lines or Shapes 3

picture of a floppy disk) on the left toolbar.

2 Press Ctrl+S after you have saved everything in the Sketchbook.

3 On the FILE menu, click Save if you have already named the file. Click Save As if you want to name the file, rename the file, or relocate the file to a different folder.

Open the Sketchbook

1 Click the View Sketchbook button on the left toolbar.

2 Press the F8 key on the keyboard.

3 On the VIEW menu, click Sketchbook.

Rotate Drawing Lines or Shapes

On the drawing worktable for either EasyDraw or Patchdraw, click the Select tool and select the line(s) or shape(s) to rotate. To select more than one, hold down the Shift key as you click to select.

1 Position your cursor on the cross arrow cursor in the middle of the shape and Ctrl+click. You will see the corners of the box outlining the line or shape turn into a curved arrow. Manually rotate the object by dragging a corner.

2 Click the dark square in the corner of the Select tool. The Symmetry menu will pop up. Choose to Rot 90, 180, or 270. You may also flip horizontally, vertically, and diagonally in two directions.

3 Position the cursor on the selected shape and right-click. The pop-out menu will include Rotate on the listing. Click Rotate and set the degrees desired. The rotation will be clockwise.

4 On the BLOCK menu, click Rotate and set the degrees desired.

Get the Pop-up Menu for the Block

1 On the BLOCK menu, click the function you want for EasyDraw or PatchDraw.

2 With your cursor on the block worktable, right-click to get the pop-up menu.

EQ4 Magic   167

Drawing a Horizontal or Vertical Grid

QUESTION

Can I use the grid tool in EasyDraw to draw just horizontal or just vertical lines?

ANSWER

Yes. If you set the number 1 for Columns and a different number for Rows, you will get only horizontal lines for your grid. Likewise, if you set the number 1 for Rows and a different number for Columns, you will get only vertical lines for your grid.

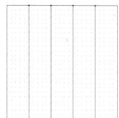

Using the Wreathmaker

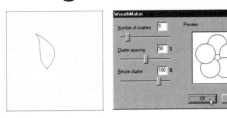

One option for Wreathmaker

Wreathmaker is one of the most fun tools since magic wands were invented. You never know for sure what you're going to get.

QUESTION

What's the easiest way to redo a wreath?

ANSWER

1   I always save the shape I'm working with in the Sketchbook. That way I can return to it as a reference.

2   With your shape on the drawing board, click the Select tool and click the shape. Right-click to get the Wreathmaker option. Make your selections in the dialog box and click OK.

3   You can always press Ctrl+Z to undo the wreath or click the EDIT menu and Undo. Select the shape again. Right-click and get the Wreathmaker dialog box back to make your changes and click OK again.

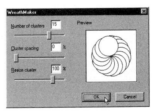

Another option for Wreathmaker

EQ4 Magic **169**

Making Templates for an On-Point Layout

When you set blocks in the On-Point quilt layout, you have the option of putting pieced blocks into the triangles around the edges or to color them as a plain block.

QUESTION

How do I get a template for the side and corner triangle plain blocks?

ANSWER

1   Set a Half-Square Triangle block or a Four X block (see EQ Libraries, 1 Classic Pieced, Simple Blocks) in the blank triangle space. Rotate the block to fill the area. The Half-Square Triangle block will give you the template for the triangles on the side of the quilt. The Four X block will give you the template for the triangles in the corners of the quilt.

2   Click the Select tool and select the block you wish to print out. On the FILE menu, click Print and Templates. For block size, check Size from quilt.

Half-Square Triangle

Four X block

Making Templates for
an On-Point Layout

Making a Country Set Grid

As much as the Country Set quilt layout is freeing because you can place blocks randomly, sometimes it's nice to be able to line things up in a grid even though you are using blocks of various shapes and/or sizes.

QUESTION

What can I use for guidelines in Country Set?

ANSWER

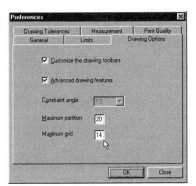

Changing maximum grid amount

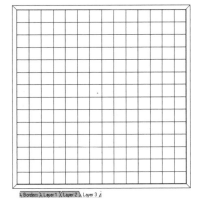

Using a grid block in a Country Set quilt layout

1 Decide what kind of a grid you want: 12 x 12, 6 x 8, or whatever. Open an EasyDraw worktable and click the dark dot in the corner of the Grid tool. Set the desired grid for columns and rows. The grid numbers go up to 14. You might need to click the FILE menu, click Preferences, click Drawing Options, and change the Maximum grid number to 14. If you need more than that to get to a number like16, for example, draw more than one 8 x 8 grid on the block. Save in Sketchbook.

2 On the Quilt Worktable, New Quilt, Country Set, go into Layout and set the preferred size of the center of your quilt. Then click Layer 3. Click the Set tool and drag a box (marquee) to fill the quilt top. Check the size and locator position boxes on the Graph Pad for accurate sizing and placement. Then click Layer 1 and set your blocks. Layer 2 can still be reserved for overlaying blocks or appliqué.

3 When you're finished with your quilt layout, click Layer 3. Click the Adjust tool. Select the grid block in Layer 3 and press Delete on your keyboard.

EQ4 Magic 171

Printing Out a Quilt

When EQ4 prints out a quilt, it fills the page as much as possible inside the margins.

QUESTION

How do I print out a smaller picture of my quilt?

ANSWER

1   One solution is to make a snapshot of your quilt on the quilt worktable and export that bitmap to a drawing program. You can size the image there and position it anywhere you like on the page.

2   Another idea is to go into the FILE menu and click Page Setup. You can change the margins for the page and control the size of the quilt printout. The quilt will print in the center of the page.

QUESTION

On the printout for my quilt, the quilt is not centered on the page. Why not?

ANSWER

Your margins may be set uneven. Go into the FILE menu and click Page Setup. Adjust the side margin settings to be even.

Printing a Line Drawing of a Quilt

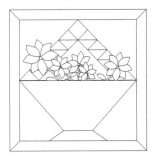

QUESTION

How do I print a line drawing of a quilt without getting any overlapping transparent shapes, as in appliqué?

ANSWER

Color the entire quilt white. Then print using the Showing fabrics option.

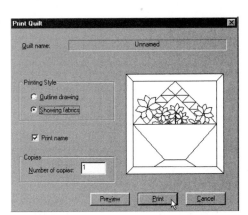

EQ4 Magic 173

Printing Foundation Patterns Grayscale

QUESTION

How do I get a foundation pattern I have drawn to print in grayscale?

ANSWER

Magic. It's all in the way you color the block. There are only four colors in the default palette that will translate to grayscale for the purpose of printing the grayscale foundation pattern. They are: black (0,0,0), dark gray (128, 128, 128), light gray (192, 192, 192) and white (255,255,255). The numbers are the RGB numbers that identify the colors. You'll see these numbers if you hold your cursor, without clicking, over a color patch on the color palette display.

Two rules to observe here:

1 The colors eligible for gray scale must be used in the *first coloring* of the block.

   If you forget and want to use grayscale for your printout after you have already colored the block, go back into the EasyDraw worktable and Save in Sketchbook another copy of the drawing of the block. Click the Color tab and use only the four colors named above for your coloring.

2 Save in Sketchbook before printing.

   Wherever you colored black, your foundation will show a dark gray. Both gray colors will be light gray in the printout. White or any other color used to color your block will be white on the printout.

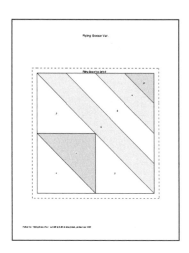

Printing Foundation Patterns Grayscale

Using EQ4 Fabrics in Other Programs

QUESTION

How do I get some of my favorite fabrics from EQ4 into other programs?

ANSWER

You can export a fabric as a plain block colored with the fabric.

Save in Sketchbook tool

Export Snapshot tool

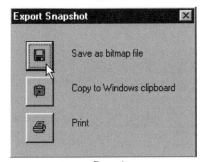

Step 4

1   On the BLOCK worktable, point to New Block and click EasyDraw. Click Save in Sketchbook and answer yes, you would like to save a blank block.

2   Click the Color tab and color the plain block with your favorite fabric. Save in Sketchbook.

3   Click the Export Snapshot tool and drag a box around your block. Keep the outline of the box slightly inside the block borders so you don't get the outline of the block.

4   Save as a bitmap. Give it a name and file it in a folder where you will find it later.

You don't need to save the project if you are using this technique just to create a bitmap file for exporting.

EQ4 Magic   175

Organizing Fabrics

QUESTION

How can I get the fabrics I use the most in a convenient place for coloring my blocks or quilts?

ANSWER

1   When the coloring palette is displayed on the Block Worktable or the Quilt Work-table, position your cursor on any fabric patch and right-click. On the pop-up menu, click Sort Fabrics. A window display of the fabrics will appear. Click the fabric that you want to appear first in the display. It will disappear. Click the other fabrics in succession. When you no longer need to discriminate about the order, click Close and the fabrics will rearrange themselves to fit your organization.

2   The fabrics will show up in the Sketchbook in the rearranged order. If there are fabrics you don't use often, you can group them at the end of your Sketchbook. You can delete fabrics. See: DELETING FABRICS FROM THE SKETCHBOOK.

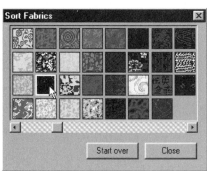

3   Once you rearrange the order of the fabrics they will stay in that position for the remainder of the time you have that EQ4 project open. Once you open a new project in EQ4 the default order will appear. To keep the fabric order that you want, open the EQ4 project where you arranged the fabrics, instantly rename it (or Save As), and begin designing your new project. Repeat this step for each new project you want the fabrics to be arranged.

🐾 **Note:**
See page 111 of the EQ4 Design Cookbook.

Deleting Fabrics from the Sketchbook

QUESTION

Is there a fast and easy way to delete fabrics from the Sketchbook?

ANSWER

1   Try this. Let's say that the first fifteen fabrics in the Sketchbook are the ones you want to delete. Open the Fabrics tab in the Sketchbook. Position your cursor on the first fabric patch in the display and click. On the keyboard, press D for Delete and then Y for Yes. As each fabric is deleted, the next in line will be highlighted in its place, and you don't have to click it again. You can click D then Y many times in succession until you have eliminated all the extraneous fabrics.

2   Don't worry about deleting fabrics that you have used in a quilt because EQ4 will warn you before you do so.

3   This is a very good practice for keeping the size of the file minimized if you have added scanned fabrics or fabrics from the Designer Libraries.

4   Once you delete fabrics they will be gone for the remainder of the time you have that EQ4 project open. Once you open a new project in EQ4 all of the default fabrics will appear. To have a project with the deleted fabrics gone, open the EQ4 project where you deleted fabrics, instantly rename it (or Save As), and begin designing your new project. Repeat this step for each new project where you do not want the deleted fabrics.

You can organize the remaining fabrics. See: ORGANIZING FABRICS.

EQ4 Magic   177

Making Wallpaper

QUESTION

How do I use blocks or quilts from EQ4 to make wallpaper for my computer?

ANSWER

1   On the main menu screen of your computer, right-click. Click Properties. The Background tab is showing. Click Browse to get access to your files. Find a bmp file that you have created from a block or a quilt or a fabric and select it. (I keep all of my EQ4 block, quilt, and fabric bmp files in a folder called "EQ4 Bitmaps" in My Documents.) Click Open.

2   Under Display, select Center (this will center the selection on your screen), Stretch* (this will fill the rectangular screen with your selection) or Tile (this will tile the selection across the screen). Click Apply. Click OK. That's it.

"Stretch" is in Windows 98 only.

3   Your wallpaper will be a graphic that is the same size as the one you saved from EQ4 or scanned or saved from web sites. If you scanned in a 2" fabric sample as a bitmap, your tiling option will use 2" tiles across your screen.

4   The size of the bitmap and your screen resolution will determine how your graphic appears on your screen.

Step 1

Saving a block as a bmp

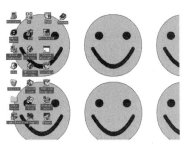

New computer wallpaper

Adding to the Help File

Adding to the Help File

QUESTION

Where can I put helpful tips for EQ4 within easy reach while using the program?

ANSWER

1   There a little known secret passageway behind the Help menu that will let you type in notes.

2   On the HELP menu, click EQ4 Help. Click the Index tab. Find a subject that relates to your intended note or comes close to the alphabetical title of your note. Scroll down the list with the scroll bar or type in a name for the search.

3   Open the subject by clicking the Display button.

4   Click EDIT on the main Help menu. Click Annotate.

5   Type in your note. Or, you could copy and paste your note from another text source. Click Save. I would recommend keeping the note short. If nothing else, you can put in a note about where to reference further information.

6   You will see a paperclip at the beginning of the text in the window. This marks where you can find your note. To open it, you will click the paper clip.

7   Click BOOKMARK on the Help menu. Click Define. Type in a title for your note and click OK.

8   The next time you go into Help and click the Index Tab and then any subject, you will be able to click Bookmark and take a shortcut to your note by selecting the title of your note.

9   It's easy to delete your note at a later time by using the Bookmark to find it, clicking the paperclip, and clicking the Delete button. In the Bookmark menu box, click the Delete button.

Step 4

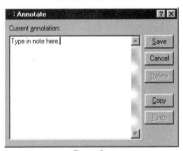

Step 5

Step 7

Type in the title of your note

Step 8

EQ4 Magic   179

Using On-Line Tech Support

QUESTION

Where do I go to get other questions answered and to learn more about using EQ4?

ANSWER

1 One of the outstanding features of Electric Quilt is the tech support. Whether it's over the phone from the Electric Quilt office or on the Internet among EQ4 users, there's an answer to every question. We're finding that the majority of Electric Quilt users have Internet access, so the Electric Quilt web site is a valuable resource. The URL is www.electricquilt.com. It's quite easy to remember.

2 At that site you will find lots of valuable information, including several links that will take you to sites set up by Electric Quilt users, who share tips and projects. You will especially want to subscribe to the Info-EQ maillist sponsored by Planet Patchwork. There are literally thousands of EQ users from around the world sharing tips on that list. The list is topic specific, and the rule is that all posts should be relevant to using Electric Quilt.

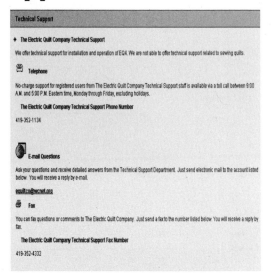

www.electricquilt.com

Organizing Tips from the Internet

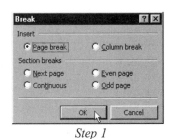

Step 1

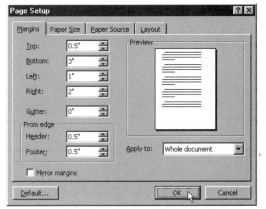

Step 2

QUESTION

What is a good way to keep track of all the tips about EQ4 that I pick up from web sites and the Info-EQ maillist?

ANSWER

1. I have a suggestion that is working for me. I copy and paste information from the Internet into a Word document that I have named "Tips and Tricks for EQ4." At the end of each tip, I click Insert, Break, Page Break, so I have only one tip on a page. For each tip, I document the source.

2. On Page Setup from the File menu, I set the margins for Top 0.5"; Bottom 3"; Left 1"; and Right 2" and apply the margins to the whole document. The printout will contain the text within those parameters.

3. The pages of the EQ4 Design Cookbook are 7" x 9". After printing out my Tips file, I trim the 8½" x 11" pages to be slightly smaller than 7" x 9" and insert them into the Cookbook close to an area of related information. I record in the lower right corner a reference page. For example, if my tip page is inserted between pages 100 and 101 of the Cookbook, I'll write 100a on my tip page. I have found more than once that that is helpful in case pages get separated from the book.

4. If my tip page contains information on a subject not already in the Cookbook, I find a good place to stick the page, number it, and make a note in the Index of the Cookbook.

5. When my Cookbook gets too fat to contain many more pages, I'll consider taking it to an office service store to get the book plus my tip pages spiral bound together.

EQ4 Magic 181

Index

Install the Free Upgrade to EQ4 on this CD

All users of EQ Version 4.0 should install the free upgrade found on this CD. This upgrade will add new features to your EQ4 program. In order to complete some of the lessons in this book, you'll need this upgrade. You do not need to worry about your current projects or library files. They will not be changed.

Checking your version of EQ

To determine what version of EQ you have, click the HELP menu in EQ4 and click About EQ4. If you have The Electric Quilt Version 4.1, the below installation is not necessary. If you have The Electric Quilt Version 4.0, continue with the instructions below. (Click OK after you are done with About EQ4.)

Installing EQ Version 4.1

Have the current version of EQ closed before continuing with this installation. To install it, place the EQ4.1 disc into your computer's CD-ROM drive. Click on the **Start** button on the task bar and choose **Run**. Type *drive letter*:**Q41SETUP** in the line labeled Open. (*For example, if the disc is in the drive D, type* ***D:\Q41SETUP***) Click the OK button and follow the instructions on your screen. (**Note:** If you do not know the letter name of your CD-ROM drive, click on the Browse button and look for the picture of the drive with the CD-ROM disc. You will see the letter name with it.)

ATTENTION! This package contains The Electric Quilt Version 4.1 Upgrade. This upgrade version of The Electric Quilt 4.1 will install only if you are a licensed user of The Electric Quilt 4.0. The installer will search your hard drive, and/or removable drive to confirm eligibility. The files on this CD package replace and supplement existing EQ4 files but do not make a full installation of EQ4.

License Agreement and Limited Warranty

By opening this sealed software CD package, you accept and agree to the terms and conditions printed below.

This software is an upgrade to The Electric Quilt Version 4 software product. You must be properly licensed for The Electric Quilt Version 4 to be eligible for this upgrade and to use it. This upgrade replaces and/or supplements The Electric Quilt Version 4 that formed the basis for your eligibility for the upgrade. You may use the resulting upgraded product only in accordance with the terms of this License Agreement.
You may use this software on a single computer, but may transfer it to another computer as long as it is used on only one computer at a time. You may make a single copy of the software for backup purposes only.
You may not lend, lease, rent, sublicense, or otherwise distribute any portion of this software. You may permanently transfer your license to use the software to another party, provided the other party agrees to accept the terms and conditions of this agreement, and that you deliver to the other party the original disc and simultaneously destroy any copy of the software in your possession. Such transfer terminates your license to use the software and any eligibility for special upgrades. The Electric Quilt Company must be notified in writing of any transfers.
The software is distributed on an "AS IS" basis without any express or implied warranties whatsoever. Because of the diversity of hardware and conditions under which this software may be used, no warranty of fitness for a particular purpose is offered. The user must assume the entire risk of using the software. Any liability of seller or manufacturer will be limited to product replacement or refund of purchase price.
Many titles used by manufacturers and sellers to distinguish their products are claimed as trademarks. Where The Electric Quilt Company was aware of these trademarks, the trademark symbol was printed beside the trademarked title or product name.
This software is protected by United State Copyright law and by International Treaty. Any use of the software in violation of these laws terminates the license and can be prosecuted.